Marketing Strategies and Strategic Marketing

Newman Enyioko

Copyright © 2014 Newman Enyioko

All rights reserved.

ISBN-13: 978-1495257490

ISBN-10: 1495257495

DEDICATION

This Book is dedicated to God Almighty for His guidance, protection, deliverance from Satan for me to reign as a king and priest here on earth. Also to my wife (Chioma) and children - Esther and Elizabeth.

REVIEW

Whether you have to undertake a course in Marketing as part of your requirements for your degree programme, or as part of your profession, or simply because you are fascinated by something you have observed and want to find out about Marketing, this book offers you advice on how to turn your ideas into a workable marketing strategies. A highly accessible style and logical structure have made this the student's choice and run-away market leader. The book is written for students in undergraduate and postgraduate degree programmes in social sciences, or business-related disciplines. Based on popular demand *Marketing Strategies and Strategic Marketing (as a* book) offers a highly accessible, clear and engaging explanations to Marketing Activities. *Marketing Strategies and Strategic Marketing* assumes no previous knowledge of the subject, and focuses on helping the reader develop a clear conceptual understanding of the nature of empirical studies in Principles of

Marketing Strategies and Strategic Marketing

Marketing and Marketing Strategies and on how those ideas lead to, and underlie, the principal Marketing techniques and profession. The eleven Ps of Marketing and their various strategic options / approaches are covered, along with practical guidance on issues such as: Concept of Marketing, Marketing Mix (11 Ps), Strategic Decisions and Consumer Behaviour, Marketing Information Systems and Marketing Research, Scope of Strategic Marketing, Marketing Planning and Environmental Analysis, Marketing Strategy, Marketing (Mix) Strategies, Strategic Market Orientation, Customer Value and Superior Performance, Marketing warfare strategies, and Relationship Marketing, Profit Impact of Marketing Strategy and B2B Marketing.

(**Barr. C.O. ONWUSORO**, LLB, M.Sc., MCITN - Facilitator Marine Policy Institute, Port Harcourt, Rivers State, Nigeria).

Newman Enyioko

CONTENTS	Page
Title Page	i
Copyright Page	ii
Dedication	iii
Book Review	iv
Table of Contents	vi
Acknowledgements	xi
Chapter 1: Meaning and Concept of Marketing Concept of Marketing	1
Marketing Mix (4 Ps)	7
Seven Ps in Marketing	9
New 4 Ps of Marketing Mix	10
Product / New Product Development	11
Product Focus	13
Pricing and Price Determination	15
Promotion (Communication Marketing)	16
Advertising	21
Distribution and Logistics	23
Concept of Physical Distribution	26
Chapter 2: Marketing Concepts, Strategic Decisions and Consumer	40
Concept / Marketing Concept	41
Production Concept	41

Product Concept	42
Selling Concept	42
Marketing Concept	42
Societal Marketing Concept	42
Strategic Planning	42
Four major characteristics/factors for High Performance Business	43
Corporate Strategic Planning	44
Consumer Behaviour	47
Stages of the Consumer Buying Process	47
Buying Decision Process	51
Types of Buying Decision	52
The Use of Herd Behaviour in Marketing	52
Customer Focus	53
The Four Elements of SIVA Model	54
Measuring and Forecasting Market Demand	55
Forecasting Methods	56
Chapter 3: Marketing Information System and Marketing Research	58
Marketing Information System	60
Value of Information	62
Marketing Research for Strategic Decision Making	64

Market Research 65
Marketing Research vs. Market Research 66
The Role and Limitations of Marketing Research 67
The Market Research Process 70
Data Types and Sources 85
Primary Data 85
Questionnaire Design 87
Measurement Scales 94
Validity and Reliability 95
Attitude Measurement 96
Sampling Plan 98
Data Collection 99
Data Analysis 100
Hypothesis Testing 101
Test of Statistical Significance 103
Chi-Square (X^2) 103
Spearman Rank Order 104
Analysis of Variance (ANOVA) 111
Discriminant Analysis 112
Factor Analysis 113
Cluster Analysis 115
Market Research Report 116

Chapter 4: Scope of Strategic Marketing 118
Understanding Marketing – Antecedents 119

Strategic Marketing Concept	126
Strategic Marketing Actions	131
Importance of Strategic Marketing	136
Responsibility in Marketing	137
Social and Ethical Constraints	139
Sources of Marketing Advantage	147
Organizational Resources and Marketing Capabilities	148
Strategic Marketing Effectiveness	151
Key Marketing Success Factors	153
Strategic Marketing Focus on Customers	153
Chapter 5: Strategic Marketing Planning and Environmental Analysis	156
Strategic vs. Tactical Marketing Plans	157
Developing the Strategic Marketing Plan	158
How to Use a Strategic Marketing Plan	159
Benefiting from a Strategic Marketing Plan	160

Marketing Plan and Business Plan	161
The Product/Service - Factors for Consideration	163
Generic Marketing Strategies	164
Pricing - Operational Strategies	166
Promotion - Operational Strategies	167
Distribution - Operational Strategies	168
The Environment	169
PEST Analysis	170
The Prospect	172
The Competition	173
Your Enterprise	174
Development	175
Production	175
Marketing/Sales	176
Market Opportunities	177
Market Segment	178
Targeting	178
Customer Services	179
Cost to Enter Market	179
Profit Potential	180
Product Launch Strategy	184
Multi- Product Resource Allocation	185

Dynamic Product Management Strategies	187
SWOT Analysis	190
Comments on the Uses of SWOT	194
Chapter 6: Marketing Strategy	199
Generic Strategies	203
Strategies for the Dominant Firms (Market Leaders)	207
Strategies for Challengers in the Industry	208
Strategies for the Followers in the Industry	210
Nicher Strategies	211
Other Conventional Corporate Strategies	213
Effective Strategy Implementation	218
Service Organisations and their Strategies	224
Strategic Options for Service Organisations	229

Chapter 7: Marketing (Mix)

Strategies	234
Product Strategy	235
Marketing Strategies in the Introduction Stage	236
Marketing Strategies in the growth stage	238
Pricing Strategy	241
Distribution Strategy	245
Types of Distribution Channels	247
Designing and Managing of Distribution Strategies	249
Promotion Strategy	253

Chapter 8 : Strategic Market Orientation, Customer

Value and Performance	259
Customer Orientation and Profitability	259
Competitor's Focus and Increased Sales Output	260
Inter functional Coordination and Superior Value	261
Quality Driven-Product and Customer Satisfaction	265
Innovation and New Product Development	266

Developing A Strategic Market Orientation	267
Alternative Approaches to Developing Strategic Market Orientation	267
Strategic Market Orientation and Continuous Learning	269

Chapter 9: Marketing warfare strategies and Relationship Marketing — 273

The Use of Marketing Warfare Strategies	273
Marketing Warfare Strategies	274
Learning from Napoleon	276
Relationship Marketing	278
Origin of the Relationship Marketing Approach	278
Usage of Relationship Marketing	278
Steps in the Relationship Marketing Process	279
Strengths (Benefits) of Relationship Marketing	279
Limitations of the Relationship Marketing model	280

Chapter 10: Profit Impact of Marketing Strategy and B2B Marketing — 282

Brief History of PIMS 282
Conclusion Drawn by PIMS 283
Participation in PIMS Study:
Costs and Benefits 284
Critique of PIMS 285
Business-To-Business 286
B2B Marketing
Communications 287
B2B Marketing
Methodologies 288
E-Marketplaces 290
Some Marketing Terms and
their Definitions 292
REFERENCES

ACKNOWLEDGEMENTS

The book is primarily intended to serve as a textbook for National Diploma, Higher National Diploma, undergraduate and graduate students in Principles of Marketing and Marketing Management disciplines of various high institutions and universities. It is hoped that the book shall provide guidelines to all interested in Principles of Marketing and Marketing Management of one sort or the other. The book is, in fact, an outgrowth of our experiences in the subject both as students and as lecturers / management consultant / researchers. I am highly indebted to our students and learned colleagues for providing the necessary stimulus for writing this book. I am grateful to all those persons whose writings and works have helped us in the preparation of this book. I am equally grateful to the reviewers of the manuscript of this book who made extreme valuable suggestions and have thus contributed in enhancing the standard of the book. I thankfully acknowledge the assistance provided by other reviewers of the manuscript of this book.

We shall feel amply rewarded if the book proves helpful in the development of Marketing Strategies. We look forward to suggestions from all readers, especially from experienced researchers and scholars for further improving the subject content as well as the presentation of this book. I am grateful to my beloved wife Mrs. Chioma Newman Enyioko and Children – Esther and Elzabeth for their patience and understanding throughout the period of writing this book. I find it impossible to make a comprehensive list of all those I should like to thank as this embraces not only my peers; but almost all my members in ANCA, The National President of ANCA, the Chairman of ANCA, Port Harcourt and FULL GOSPEL Businessmen Fellowship International D/Line Model and Central Chapters as well as the Pastors and Prayer Force members of Living Faith CHURCH, Kaduna Street D/Line Port Harcourt. I thank my friends UZONDU, PHILIP, VICTOR OKORO, Simeon Nwandu, Victor Okoro, Barr. Onwukwe, Barr. Onwusoro, Dr. Dan and Hon. Chief Chidi Lloyd (Esq). My grateful acknowledgement is made to my mother Mrs Rodah Mgbeahuru Enyioko

Marketing Strategies and Strategic Marketing

for her great inspiration and encouragement in times when my mind is wearied. I thank my brothers and sisters as well as my in-laws for the understanding.

PREFACE

This Book, organized in ten chapters succinctly covers topical and critical issues in Marketing Management and Strategies. Chapter 1 x-rays the Meaning and Concept of Marketing, Marketing Mix (4 Ps), Seven Ps in Marketing and New 4 Ps of Marketing Mix. Chapter 2 examines Marketing Concepts, Strategic Decisions and Consumer, Production Concept, Product Concept, Selling Concept, Societal Marketing Concept, Strategic Planning, Four major characteristics/factors for High Performance Business, Corporate Strategic Planning, Consumer Behaviour, Stages of the Consumer Buying Process, Types of Buying Decision, The Use of Herd Behaviour in Marketing, Customer Focus, The Four Elements of SIVA Mode, Measuring and Forecasting. Market Demand and Forecasting Methods. The Chapter 3 of the book covers Marketing Information Systems and Marketing Research, Value of Information, Marketing Research for Strategic Decision Making Market Research, Marketing Research versus Market Research, The Role and Limitations of Marketing Research, The

Marketing Strategies and Strategic Marketing

Market Research Process, Data Types and Sources, Primary Data, Questionnaire Design, Measurement Scales, Validity and Reliability, Attitude Measurement, Sampling Plan, Data Collection, Data Analysis, Hypothesis Testing, Test of Statistical Significance, Chi-Square (X^2), Spearman Rank Order, Analysis of Variance (ANOVA), Discriminant Analysis, Factor Analysis, Cluster Analysis and Market Research Report . Chapter 4 investigates the Scope of Strategic Marketing, Understanding Marketing – Antecedents, Strategic Marketing Concept, Strategic Marketing Actions, Importance of Strategic Marketing, Responsibility in Marketing, Social and Ethical Constraints, Sources of Marketing Advantage, Organizational Resources and Marketing Capabilities, Strategic Marketing Effectiveness, Key Marketing Success Factors and Strategic Marketing Focus on Customers. Chapter 5 explores Strategic Marketing Planning and Environmental Analysis, Strategic versus Tactical Marketing Plans, Developing the Strategic Marketing Plan, How to Use a Strategic Marketing Plan, Benefiting from a Strategic Marketing Plan, Marketing Plan and Business Plan, The Product/Service -Factors for Consideration, Generic Marketing Strategies, Pricing - Operational Strategies, Promotion - Operational Strategies, Distribution - Operational Strategies, The Environment , PEST Analysis, Market Opportunities, Market Segment, Customer Services, Cost to Enter Market, Profit Potential, Product Launch Strategy, Multi- Product Resource Allocation, Dynamic Product Management Strategies and SWOT Analysis. Chapter 6 x-rays Marketing Strategy, Generic Strategies, Strategies for the Dominant Firms (Market Leaders), Strategies for Challengers in the Industry, Strategies for the Followers in the Industry, Nicher Strategies , Other Conventional Corporate Strategies, Effective Strategy Implementation, Service Organisations and their Strategies. Chapter 7 of the Book examines Marketing (Mix) Strategies, Product Strategy, Marketing Strategies in the Introduction Stage, Marketing Strategies in the growth stage, Pricing Strategy, Distribution Strategy, Types of Distribution Channels, Designing and Managing of Distribution Strategies and Promotion

Strategy. Chapter 8 discusses issues concerning Strategic Market Orientation, Customer Value and Performance, Customer Orientation and Profitability, Competitor's Focus and Increased Sales Output, Inter functional Coordination and Superior Value, Quality Driven-Product and Customer Satisfaction, Innovation and New Product Development, Developing A Strategic Market Orientation, Alternative Approaches to Developing Strategic Market Orientation, Strategic Market Orientation and Continuous Learning . Chapter 9 examines Marketing warfare Strategies and Relationship Marketing, the Use of Marketing Warfare Strategies, Marketing Warfare Strategies, Learning from Napoleon, Relationship Marketing, Origin of the Relationship Marketing Approach, Usage of Relationship Marketing, Steps in the Relationship Marketing Process, Strengths (Benefits) of Relationship Marketing and Limitations of the Relationship Marketing model. The Book ends with Chapter 10 covering such topics as Profit Impact of Marketing Strategy and B2B Marketing, Brief History of PIMS, Conclusion Drawn by PIMS, Participation in

Newman Enyioko

PIMS Study in Costs and Benefits, Critique of PIMS, Business-To-Business, B2B Marketing Communications, B2B Marketing Methodologies, E-Marketplaces as well as Some Marketing Terms and their Definitions.

CHAPTER 1

MEANING AND CONCEPT OF MARKETING

Concept of Marketing

Marketing has been conceptualized and defined in various ways by many authorities. It involves assembling the required goods and services and exchanging them profitably with considerations to customers who buy for satisfaction of their wants and needs. The British Institute of Marketing (BIMARK) cited by Appleby, (1969: 181) defines marketing thus: *The creative management function which promotes trade and employment by assessing consumer needs and initiating research and development to meet them. It coordinates resources of production and distribution of the goods and services, determines and directs the nature of the total efforts required to sell profitably the maximum production to the ultimate user.*

This definition sees marketing in consonance with what Drucker, (1965) calls creative function. He maintains that the concept of marketing is so basic in anybusiness organisation that it cannot be considered as a separate function in an establishment. It is the whole business seen from the point of view of its final result, that is, the customer point of view. In fact, business success is determined by marketing activities because of this creative function of marketing. A definition given by Onah, (1979) sees marketing as the business process by which production and services are matched with market and through transfer of ownership so as to maximize long term earnings per share.

Kotler, (1994:6) in his own definition opines that marketing is a social and managerial process by which individuals and groups obtain what they need and want through creating and exchanging products of value with others. This definition of marketing as outlined by Kotler, (1994) rests on the following core concepts:

- Needs
- Wants, and
- Demand;
- Product
- Value
- Cost, and
- Satisfaction;
- Exchange
- Transaction and relationships
- Markets and Marketing.

Exchange plays very vital role in marketing and as such certain conditions must be met before it takes place. The five conditions necessary for exchange to take place are:

- there must be at least two parties
- each party has something that might be of value to the other.
- each party believes it is appropriate or desirable to deal with the other party and
- each party is free to accept or reject the offer.

Also, Hamermesh, (1984: 1) defines marketing as: *The total system of interacting business activities designed to plan, price, promote and distribute want satisfying product and services to present and potential customers.*

This definition centres on how effectively and efficiently the organisation is able to use its marketing mix (4Ps) to achieve its aims and objectives. For the purpose of small business, Siropolis, (1994: 424) defines marketing as "the effort to identify and satisfy customer's needs and wants". This definition sees the customer as the central focus of marketing. How do we identify the needs of the customer? So that we can prepare products and services at appropriate prices and promote them effectively with good delivery arrangement in order to satisfy them. When we have done these things our customers would be happy to pay us some considerations in exchange and we would have achieved our organisational objectives. This is our own point of view about marketing for which we would encourage business operators to adopt.

Marketing is a societal process which discerns consumers' wants, focusing on a product or service to fulfil those wants, attempting to mould the consumers toward the products or services offered. Marketing is fundamental to any businesses growth. The marketing teams (marketers) are tasked to create consumer awareness of the products or services through marketing techniques. Unless it pays due attention to its products and services and consumers' demographics and desires, a business will not usually prosper over time.

Marketing tends to be seen as a creative industry, which includes advertising, distribution and selling. It is also concerned with anticipating the customers' future needs and wants, which are often discovered through market research.

Essentially, marketing is the process of creating or directing an organization to be successful in selling a product or service that people not only desire, but are willing to buy.

Therefore good marketing must be able to create a "proposition" or set of benefits for the end customer that delivers value through products or services.

Its specialist areas include:

- advertising and branding
- communications
- database marketing
- direct Marketing
- event organization
- global marketing
- international marketing
- internet marketing
- industrial marketing
- market research
- public relations
- retailing
- search engine marketing
- marketing strategy
- marketing plan
- strategic management.

A market-focused, or customer-focused, organization first determines what its potential customers' desire, and then builds the **product** or service. Marketing theory / practice is justified in the belief that **customers** use a product or service because they have a need, or because it provides a perceived benefit.

Marketing Strategies and Strategic Marketing

Two major factors of marketing are the recruitment of new customers (acquisition) and the retention and expansion of relationships with existing customers (base management). Once a marketer has converted the prospective buyer, base management marketing takes over. The process for base management shifts the marketer to building a relationship, nurturing the links, enhancing the benefits that sold the buyer in the first place, and improving the product/service continuously to protect the business from competitive encroachments, hence the need for marketing strategies (Okwandu,1998).

For a marketing plan to be successful, the mix of the four "Ps" must reflect the wants and desires of the consumer s or Shoppers in the target market. Trying to convince a market segment to buy something they don't want is extremely expensive and seldom successful. Marketers depend on insights from marketing research, both formal and informal, to determine what consumers want and what they are willing to pay for it. Marketers hope that this process will give them a sustainable competitive advantage. Marketing Management is the practical application of this process. The offer is also an important addition to the 4Ps' theory.

Within most organizations, the activities encompassed by the marketing function are led by a Vice President or Director of Marketing. A growing number of organizations, especially large companies, have a Chief Marketing Officer position, reporting to the Chief Executive Officer.

The American Marketing Association (AMA, 1960) states that: "Marketing is the activity, set of institutions, and processes for creating, communicating, delivering, and exchanging offerings that have value for customers, clients, partners, and society at large.".

Marketing methods are informed by many of the social sciences, particularly psychology, sociology, and economics. Anthropology is also a small, but growing influence. Market research underpins these activities. Through advertising, it is also related to many of the creative arts. Marketing is a wide and heavily interconnected subject with extensive publications. It is also an area of activity infamous for re-inventing itself and its vocabulary according to the times and the culture.

Two Levels of Marketing

Strategic Marketing attempts to determine how an organization competes against its competitors in a market place. In particular, it aims at generating a competitive advantage relative to its competitors.

Operational Marketing executes marketing functions to attract and keep customers and to maximize the value derived for them, as well as to satisfy the customer with prompt services and meeting the customer expectations. Operational Marketing includes the determination of the marketing mix (4 Ps).

Marketing Mix (Four Ps)

In the early 1960's, Professor Neil Borden at Harvard Business School identified a number of company performance actions that can influence the consumer decision to purchase goods or services. Borden suggested that all those actions of the company represented a "Marketing Mix". Professor E. Jerome McCarthy, also at the Harvard Business School in the early 1960s, suggested that the Marketing Mix contained 4 elements: product, price, promotion and place.

In popular usage, "marketing" is the promotion of products, especially advertising and branding. However, in professional usage the term has a wider meaning which recognizes that marketing is customer-centred. Products are often developed to meet the desires of groups of customers or even, in some cases, for specific customers. E. Jerome McCarthy divided marketing into four general sets of activities. His typology has become so universally recognized that his four activity sets, the Four Ps, have passed into the language (McCarthy, 1984).

The four Ps are:

- *Product*: The product aspects of marketing deal with the specifications of the actual goods or services, and how it relates to the end-user's needs and wants. The scope of a product generally includes supporting elements such as warranties, guarantees, and support.
- *Pricing*: This refers to the process of setting a price for a product, including discounts. The price need not be monetary - it can simply be what is exchanged for the product or services, e.g. time, energy, psychology or attention.

- *Promotion*: This includes advertising, sales promotion, publicity, and personal selling, branding and refers to the various methods of promoting the product, brand, or company.
- *Place* (or distribution): refers to how the product gets to the customer; for example, point of sale placement or retailing. This fourth P has also sometimes been called *Place*, referring to the channel by which a product or services is sold (e.g. online vs. retail), which geographic region or industry, to which segment (young adults, families, business people), etc.

These four elements are often referred to as the marketing mix by, McCarthy, (1984) which a marketer can use to craft a marketing plan. The four Ps model is most useful when marketing low value consumer products. Industrial products, services, high value consumer products require adjustments to this model. Services marketing must account for the unique nature of services. Industrial or B2B marketing must account for the long term contractual agreements that are typical in supply chain transactions. Relationship marketing attempts to do this by looking at marketing from a long term relationship perspective rather than individual transactions.

As a counter to this, Morgan, in *Riding the Waves of Change* (Jossey-Bass, 1988), suggests that one of the greatest limitations of the 4 Ps approach "is that it unconsciously emphasizes the inside–out view (looking from the company outwards), whereas the essence of marketing should be the outside–in approach". Nevertheless, the 4 Ps offer a memorable and workable guide to the major categories of marketing activity, as well as a framework within which these can be used.

Seven Ps in Marketing

As well as the standard four Ps (Product, Pricing, Promotion and Place), services marketing calls for extra three Ps, totalling seven and known together as the extended marketing mix. These are:

- *People*: Any person coming into contact with customers can have an impact on overall satisfaction. Whether as part of a supporting service to a product or involved in a total service, people are particularly important because, in the customer's eyes, they are generally inseparable from the total service . As a result of this, they must be appropriately trained, well motivated and the right type of person. Fellow customers are also sometimes referred to under 'people', as they too can affect the customer's service experience, (e.g., at a sporting event).
- *Process*: This is the process involved in providing a service and the behaviour of people, which can be crucial to customer satisfaction.
- *Physical evidence*: Unlike a product, a service cannot be experienced before it is delivered, which makes it intangible. This, therefore, means that potential customers could perceive greater risk when deciding whether to use a service. To reduce the feeling of risk, thus improving the chance for success, it is often vital to offer potential customers the chance to see what a service would be like. This is done by providing physical

evidence, such as case studies, testimonials or demonstrations (Brown, 1998).

New Four Ps of Marketing Mix

- Personalization: It is here referred to customization of products and services through the use of the Internet. Early examples include Dell on-line and Amazon.com, but this concept is further extended with emerging social media and advanced algorithms. Emerging technologies will continue to push this idea forward.

- Participation: This is to allow customer to participate in what the brand should stand for; what should be the product directions and even which ads to run. This concept is laying the foundation for disruptive change through democratization of information.

- Peer-to-Peer: This refers to customer networks and communities where advocacy happens. The historical problem with marketing is that it is "interruptive" in nature, trying to impose a brand on the customer. This is most apparent in TV advertising. These "passive customer bases" will ultimately be replaced by the "active customer communities". Brand engagement happens within those conversations. P2P is now being referred as Social Computing and will likely to be the most disruptive force in the future of marketing.

- Predictive Modelling: This refers to neutral network algorithms that are being successfully applied in marketing problems (both a regression as well as a classification problem).

Product

New Product Development

Scope

- Breadth -- number of product lines in a range.
- Depth -- number of product items in a product line.

Steps in Product Design

- Design and development of product ideas.
- Selection of and sifting through product ideas.
- Design and testing of product concept.
- Analysis of profitability of product concept.
- Design and testing of physical product.

Packaging

Packaging and Labelling

Requirements of good packaging

- Functional - effectively contain and protect the contents
- Provide convenience during distribution, sale, opening, use, reuse, etc.
- Be environmentally responsible
- Be cost effective
- Appropriately designed for target market

- Eye-catching (particularly for retail/consumer sales)
- Communicate attributes and recommended use of the product and package
- Compliant with retailers' requirements
- Promotes image of enterprise
- Distinguishable from competitors' products
- Meet legal requirements for product and packaging
- Point of difference in service and supply of product.
- For a perfect product, perfect colour.

Forms of Packaging

- Specialty packaging — emphasizes the elegant character of the product
- Packaging for double-use
- Combination packaging two or more products packaged in the same container
- Kaleidoscopic packaging — packaging changes continually to reflect a series or particular theme
- Packaging for immediate consumption — to be thrown away after use
- Packaging for resale — packed, into appropriate quantities, for the retailer or wholesaler Trademarks

Trademark
Significance of a Trademark

- Distinguishes one company's goods from those of another
- Serves as advertisement for quality

- Protects both consumers and manufacturers
- Used in displays and advertising campaigns
- Used to market new products

Requirements of a Good Trademark

- Reflects products' advantages
- Good, simple language
- Easily pronounced and remembered
- Distinct from names of other products
- Easily added to an existing range
- Easily registered for legal protection

Brand

A brand is a name, term, design, symbol, or other feature that distinguishes products and services from competitive offerings. A brand represents the consumers' experience with an organization, product, or service.

Product Focus

In a product innovation approach, the company pursues product innovation, then tries to develop a market for the product. Product innovation drives the process and marketing research is conducted primarily to ensure that a profitable market segment(s) exists for the innovation. The rationale is that customers may not know what options will be available to them in the future so we should not expect them to tell us what they will buy in the future. However, marketers can aggressively over-pursue product innovation and try to overcapitalize on a niche. When pursuing a product innovation approach, marketers must ensure that they have a varied and multi-tiered approach to product innovation. It is claimed that if

Thomas Edison depended on marketing research he would have produced larger candles rather than inventing light bulbs. Many firms, such as research and development focused companies, successfully focus on product innovation (Such as Nintendo who constantly change the way Video games are played). Many purists doubt whether this is really a form of marketing orientation at all, because of the ex post status of consumer research. Some even question whether it is marketing.

- An emerging area of study and practice concerns internal marketing, or how employees are trained and managed to deliver the brand in a way that positively impacts the acquisition and retention of customers (employer branding).

- Diffusion of innovations research explores how and why people adopt new products, services and ideas.

- A relatively new form of marketing uses the Internet is called internet marketing or more generally e-marketing, affiliate marketing, desktop advertising or online marketing. It typically tries to perfect the segmentation strategy used in traditional marketing. It targets its audience more precisely, and is sometimes called personalized marketing or one-to-one marketing.

- With consumers' eroding attention span and willingness to give time to advertising messages, marketers are turning to forms of Permission marketing such as Branded content, Custom media and Reality marketing.

Pricing

Pricing refers to the amount of money exchanged for a product. This value is determined by utility to the consumer in terms of money and/or sacrifice that he is prepared to give for it.

Objectives

- Definite sales volume
- Achieve profit
- Larger market share
- Maintain market share
- Eliminate competition
- Advantages of mass production

Factors Influencing Price-determination

- Production and distribution costs
- Substitute goods available
- Normal trade practices
- Fixed prices
- Reaction of distributors
- Reaction of consumers
- Nature of demand:
    - Elastic
    - Inelastic
- Form of market:
    - Perfect competition
    - Monopolistic competition

- Monopoly
- Oligopoly
- philosophy

Steps to Determine Price

- Determine market share to be captured
- Set up price strategy
- Estimate demand
- Evaluate competitors' reactions.

Promotion (Communication Marketing)

Due to increased competition, privatisation and globalisation, marketing and business development have become increasingly important functions in all construction organisations. Marketing research, branding and public relations are increasingly being seen as vital in a marketplace typified by sophisticated and demanding clients and customers, and a socially and environmentally aware general public and media.

Criticism of Marketing

Some aspects of marketing, especially promotion, are the subject of criticism. It is especially problematic in classical economic theory, which is based on the assumption that supply and demand are independent. However, product promotion is an attempt coming from the supply side to influence demand. In this way producer market power is attained as measured by profits that would not be realized under a free market. Then the argument follows that non-free markets are imperfect and lead to production and consumption of suboptimal amounts of the product.

Critics acknowledge that marketing has legitimate uses in connecting goods and services to the consumers who want them. Critics also point out that marketing techniques have been used to achieve morally dubious ends by businesses, governments and criminals. Critics see a systemic social evil inherent in marketing (Hambrick, Donald, Fredrickson and James 2001). Marketing is accused of creating ruthless exploitation of both consumers and workers by treating people as commodities whose purpose is to consume. Most marketers believe that marketing techniques themselves are amoral. While it is ethically neutral, it can be used for negative purposes, such as selling unhealthy food to obese people or selling SUVs in a time of global warming, but it can also have a positive influence on consumer welfare (Brown, 1998).

The Observer's survey among 1,206 UK adult consumers in 2001 highlighted some of the stark changes our society has gone through in the last two decades. This raises a question on the effectiveness of the CIM's definition of marketing (anticipating, identifying and satisfying customer needs profitably), mainly in consumer marketing. There are similar concerns in industrial markets, also known as business-to-business or B2B. Industrial market segmentation attempts to provide some answers.

Core marketing elements such as segmentation, targeting and positioning are still relevant in the modern (or post-modern) world (Kotler, 1994). However, they are complex topics that need a high level of effort, intelligent thinking as well as resources to be implemented successfully. A definitive statement cannot be made whether the conventional marketing concept is applicable in today's environment. Its relevance is very much situational and depends on many factors such as the product, the segment, time, location, political and economic conditions and the inner workings of a company. However, some scholars such as Stephen Brown challenge the marketing concept in an extreme language. Their statements, sometimes unfair, are relevant, which is why Post-Modern Marketing was chosen as a key reference point for this chapter (Brown, 1998).

On the one hand Brown makes positive statements about marketing, e.g. "marketing is endowed with considerable personal charm and has enjoyed more than its fair share of conquests" (Brown, 1998:16); and "indeed, the increasing academic attention that is being devoted to marketing and consumption-related phenomena by non-business disciplines such as sociology, anthropology and history; far from being the second-hand rose of the scholarship, marketing is now something of a fashion leader" (Brown, 1998:17). On the other hand, he condemns marketing by saying "marketing has to decide whether to expose its intellectual nakedness or press itself against the searing heat of postmodernism" (p 17); and using phrases such as "mid-life crisis" (p 23); "in decline; failing; anachronistic; being abandoned; no longer appropriate; in an unprecedented state of crisis; delivered nothing of value; failure; confusion; misunderstanding; occasional inexplicable hitting of the jackpot" (p. 21).

This apparent love-hate relationship is proof in itself that even a sceptics find it difficult to deny the contribution that marketing has made and can make to customer satisfaction and economic value. It has contributed to both customers' and suppliers' quality of life by selecting profitable customer satisfaction as its sole objective. The marketing concept, together with other business disciplines, helped the UK to make the transition from a 19th-century manufacturing economy to a modern model of success in the service industry, creating an economic growth period never seen before in the United Kingdom (Harrigan, 1980).

Marketing has helped create value through customized products, no-questions-asked refund policies, comfortable cars, environmental attention, shopkeepers' smile, and guaranteed delivery dates. Even some government departments address the public not as 'the Queen's subjects' or 'the applicants' any more but as 'customers.' Of course all of the above is done for economic or political gain, for better or worse. Despite all this achievement, to dismiss marketing as a failure is unfair (Kotler, 1994). Marketing also helps companies avoid unnecessary R&D, operational and sales costs by helping to develop products because customers want them, not for the sake of innovation. Another success is the now commonly implemented value-pricing principle, whereby a product or service is sold for the price the customer is willing to pay, not on a cost-plus basis. This way, both suppliers and customers get a fair deal. (Kotler, 1994).

In the context of segmentation, Brown suggests that "the traditional, linear, step-by-step marketing model of analysis, planning, implementation and control no longer seems applicable, appropriate or even pertinent to what is actually happening on the ground" (p. 23-24). If Mr. Brown had studied "the ground" before making his statement, he would have realised that companies are successful the world over precisely because they implement this model.

They segment their markets, relate their products and services to them, define their value proposition and serve their customers accordingly. Examples are General Electric, HSBC, PriceWaterhouseCoopers, Smiths Aerospace, BAE Systems, BOC Edwards, Weir Group and the BT Group to name but a few. A brief visit to their websites can make this point clear.

Stephen Brown also has a constructive suggestion: "I reckon we need more passion in marketing, not less; it is time we banished banishing passion from works of marketing scholarship" (p. 256). This refers mainly to promotion, which is only one element within the marketing concept. The truth is that marketing today leads the way in segmentation, innovation, pricing, product management, distribution, and last but not least, promotion.

Marketing Communications

Marketing communications breaks down the strategies involved with marketing messages into categories based on the goals of each message. There are distinct stages in converting strangers to customers that govern the communication medium that should be used.

Advertising

- Paid form of public presentation and expressive promotion of ideas
- Aimed at masses
- Manufacturer may determine what goes into advertisement
- Pervasive and impersonal medium

Functions and advantages of successful advertising

- Task of the salesman made easier
- Forces manufacturer to live up to conveyed image
- Protects and warns customers against false claims and inferior products
- Enables manufacturer to mass-produce product
- Continuous reminder
- Uninterrupted production a possibility
- Increases goodwill
- Raises standards of living (or perceptions thereof)
- Prices decrease with increased popularity
- Educates manufacturer and wholesaler about competitors' offerings as well as shortcomings in their own.

Objectives

- Maintain demand for well-known goods
- Introduce new and unknown goods
- Increase demand for well-known goods

Requirements of a good advertisement

- Attract attention
- Stimulate interest

- Create a desire
- Bring about action
- Create Awareness

Eight steps in an advertising campaign

- Market research
- Setting out aims
- Budgeting
- Choice of media (TV, newspaper ,radio)
- Choice of actors (New Trend)
- Design and wording
- Coordination
- Test results

Personal sales

Oral presentation given by a salesman who approaches individuals or a group of potential customers:

- Live, interactive relationship
- Personal interest
- Attention and response

Sales promotion

Short-term incentives to encourage buying of products:

- Instant appeal
- Anxiety to sell

Publicity

- Stimulation of demand through press release giving a favourable report to a product
- Higher degree of credibility
- Effectively news
- Boosts enterprise's image

Distribution (Distribution and Logistics) Distribution and logistics are used inter-changeably to mean the same thing. However, distribution could be used generally to mean the coordinated approach to movement of goods and services from the producer to the consumer. It is seen by Schewe, (2000:386) "as a means that involves the movement of products in all stages of development from resource procurement through manufacturing and onto final sales". A product or service that is priced must be made available to buyers for the exchange to occur and this is where distribution comes to play prominent roles. In fact, placing goods and services where they are needed and when they are wanted constitute the business activity called distribution. In this context, distribution is used to cover integrated activities and functions needed to move goods and services from the point of production to the point of consumption. In this understanding it involves inventory and warehousing, transportation, scheduling and customer services (Enyioko, 2005). According to Corey, (2003:263): A distribution system is a key external resource. Normally, it takes years to build, and it is not easily changed. It ranks in importance with key internal resources such as manufacturing research, engineering, and field sales personnel and facilities. It represents a significant corporate commitment to large number of independent companies whose business is distribution and to the particular markets they serve. It represents, as well, a commitment to a set of policies and practices that constitute the basic fabric on which is woven an extensive set to long-term relationships. Distribution area of marketing involves strategic and tactical decision as Schewe, (2000), observes. The strategic decision involves choosing a distribution channel and the intermediaries that will make up the system for moving the products to the market. While the tactical decision involves the choice of exactly which firm to be used as intermediaries and how actual movement of products/services will take place. We have highlighted the strategic criteria in designing and managing of distribution channels (pp22-26). On the other hand, logistics is mostly used to mean movement and transportation. In business it is mostly applied under operations and research areas. As Koontz, et al (1980) observe, logistic model is "essentially a model which treats the entire materials flow system of a business from sales forecast through purchasing and processing materials and inventorying them to shipping finished goods to a company's sales warehouses – as single system". Logistics is concerned with the shipment of goods and services and movement of people from one destination to another (Enyioko, 2005). As highlighted by Koontz, et al (1980) logistics is seen in operation research as "distribution logistics model". Figure 1.1 shows the distribution logistics model.

Marketing Strategies and Strategic Marketing

Figure 1.1: Distribution Logistics Model

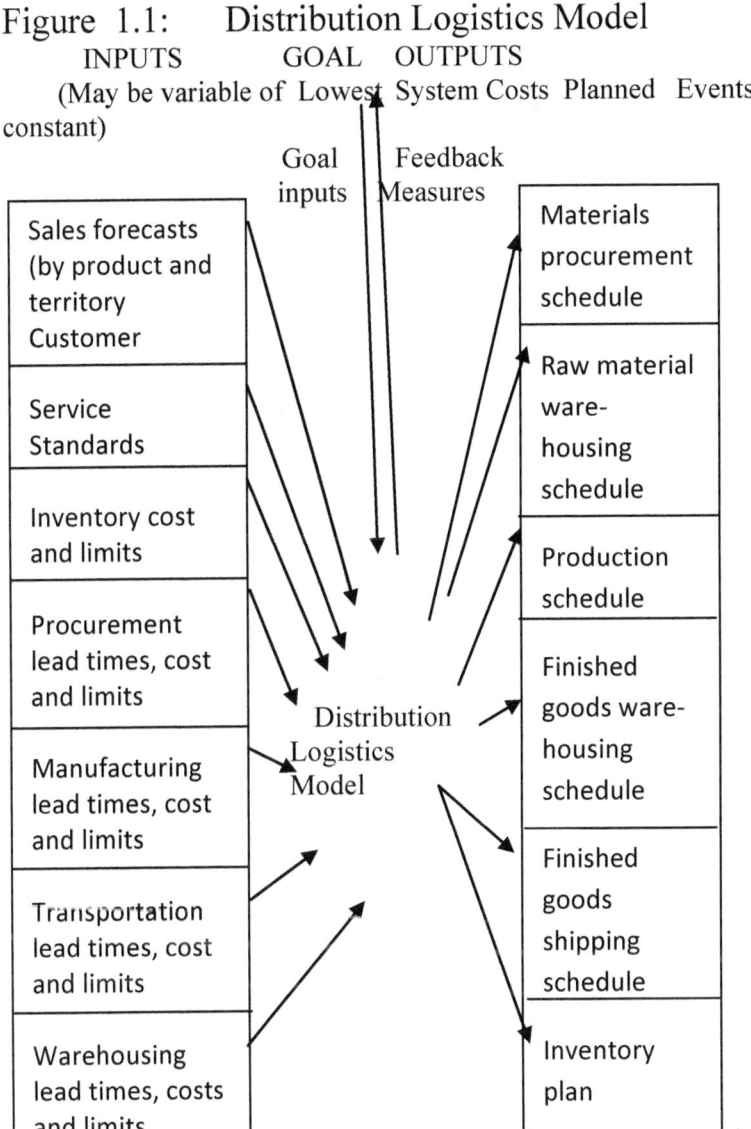

Source: Koontz, et al. (1980): Management Seventh edition. Tokyo McGraw-Hill International, (P. 25). The distribution logistics model shows the relationships between the goal desired, the input variables and limits, and the expected outputs. The organization represented by this model is a consumer goods manufacturing company with a fairly broad line of products, a number of plants (some producing the whole line, others producing only part of the line). The system would require fast feedback for control, good sales forecasting and required distribution managers able to override the system by quick change. A fully developed distribution logistics system is a fine instrument of planning and control. As further highlighted by Koontz et al, (1980) one of the most exciting logistics in planning and control is in the expression of inventory control to include other factors, referred to here as "distribution logistics". This treats the entire logistics of a business – from sales forecast through purchase and processing of materials, inventory to shipping of the finished goods. The goal of distribution logistics as a single system is usually to optimize production and reduce the total costs in the system.

Concept of Physical Distribution
Physical distribution is a key ingredient in movement of physical products including the warehousing and transportation aspects of the products. Manufacturers are constantly occupied with the ways and means of storing their wares and transporting them to the required destinations for disposal. The function of physical distribution is to see that the products are well preserved or stored and transported effectively and efficiently with minimal cost arrangement to the appropriate places of disposal or consumption. In essence as Kotler, (2005) hinted, producers of physical products and services must decide on the best possible arrangement for storing and movement of their goods to market destinations.

According to Schewe (2000:457) physical distribution function consists of all the activities that provide for efficient flow of raw materials in process inventory and finished goods from the point of procurement to the ultimate consumer.

This definition recognizes the movement of raw materials to the point of production and processing to same. The physical system is responsible for actually moving of products in such a way as to accomplish the goal of time, and place utility. The objective of physical distribution is summed up in a statement by Robert Woodnuff, former president of Coca-cola: "Our policy is to put Coke within an arm's length of desire". (Perreanet Jr. et al, 2002:3-10). Physical distribution sees that the required quantity of goods and services are brought to the right place at the appropriate time with right pricing arrangement to the customer. Enioto, (2005) opines that physical distribution could sometimes be described as logistics as it is involved in physical flow of products from producers to consumers. However, Enyioko, (2005) in his own argument maintains that the only difference between logistics and physical distribution is that, logistics integrates the movement of people with the shipment of goods and services to a given destination, but physical distribution emphasizes the procurement of materials for production, the storing of inventories and the shipment of the finished goods to market place for sale.

The American National Council of physical distribution management (1969:10) defines physical distribution as: A term employed in manufacturing and commerce to describe the broad range of activities concerned with efficient movement of finished products from the end of the production line to the consumer and in some cases include movement of raw materials from the source of supply to the beginning of the production line. These activities include freight, transportation, warehousing, material handling, protective packaging, inventory control plant and warehouse site selection, order processing, market forecasting and customer services.

From the stand point of this definition it is very clear that the main objective of physical distribution is to get the right quantity of goods placed at the reach of the customer at the required time. The economic impact of physical distribution is enormous as it accounts for over 20% of marketing costs in most organizations, (Schewe, 2005).

Kotler, (2005:585) says that physical distribution "involves planning, implementing and controlling the physical flow of materials and final goods from point of origin to point of use to meet customer requirements at a profit." He maintains that the aim of physical distribution is to manage supply chains that is, value added flow from suppliers to ultimate users. The process of physical distribution flow management is shown in figure 1.2.

Figure 1.2 Physical Distribution Flow

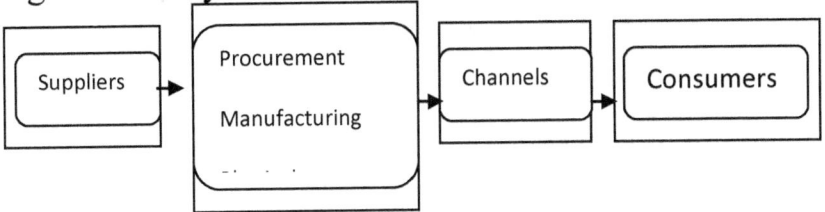

Source: Kotler, (2005:585) Marketing Management, Analysis Planning Implementation and Control 8th Edition New Jersey Prentice Hall Inc.

The logistical task of physical distribution is to co-ordinate the activities of suppliers, purchasing agents, marketers, channel members and customers. As equally highlighted by Kotler, (2005) physical distribution involves several activities as could be seen in figure 1.3

Figure 1.3: Major Activities involved in Physical Distribution

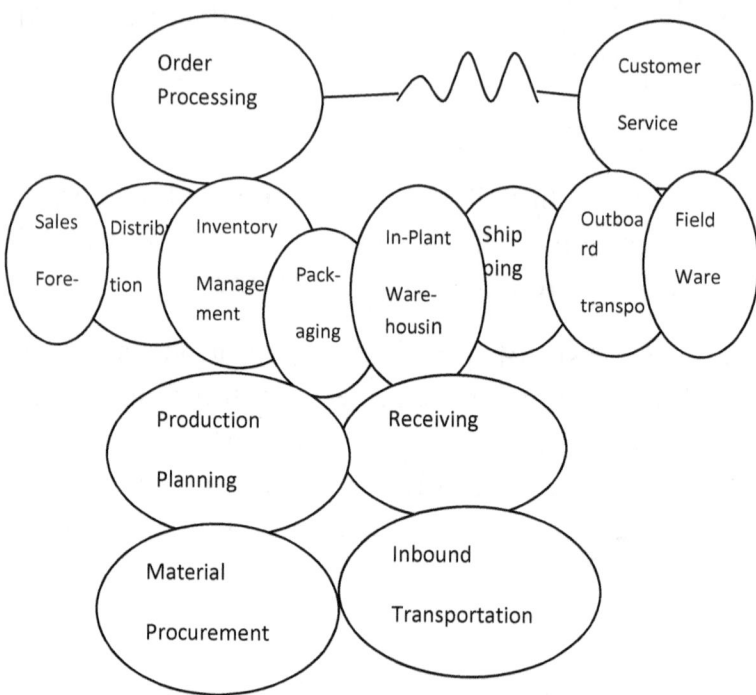

Source: Adapted from Kotler, (2005:58) with amendment to meet environmental needs.

From figure 1.3 above, we have seen that physical distribution is involved with several activities. The first is forecasting of sales, on the basis of which the company schedules production and inventory levels. The production plan indicates the materials that the purchasing department must order. These materials arrive through in-bond transportation enter the receiving area and are stored in raw material inventory. Raw materials are converted into finished goods. Finished goods inventory is the link between the customer's orders and the company's manufacturing activity. Customers' order draw down the finished goods inventory level and manufacturing activity builds it up. Finished goods flow off the assembly line and pass through packing, in-plant warehousing, shipping room processing, out bond transportation, field warehousing and customer delivery and servicing (Kotler, 2005).

As earlier indicated the main objective of physical distribution is to get the right quantity of products reach the door of the customer at the right place and time Schewe, (2005) adds that the main goal of physical distribution is to "ensure that the right products are available when consumers want them – in the right place at the right time". He further outlined the objectives of physical distribution to include:

- Availability: suppliers at each point in the distribution arrangement must anticipate demand be prepared to furnish and supply all items ordered by customers.

- Accurate Order Filling: Orders made by customers should be filled appropriately by channel members responsible in order to reach the customer appropriately too.

- Delivery of Undamaged Goods: Physical distribution must also pay attention to all activities that could cause damage to goods – materials handling procedures, packaging, storage and mode of transportation.

- Speedy and Reliable Delivery: Physical distribution activities must be performed between the time when a need or product is recognized by a channel member and the time when those products are received.

In further explanations as to the objectives of physical distribution Kotler, (2005:588) opines that it is as simple "as getting the right goods to the right place at the right time for the least cost". The least cost issue is the main critical point in physical distribution decision. In order to satisfy the customers' distribution needs with least cost arrangement certain salient issues are normally brought into focus. These critical decision areas that need proper examination and analysis include:

- How should orders be handled? Order Processing.
- Where should stocks or wares be located? Warehousing
- How much stock should be held? Inventory.
- How should goods be shipped? Transportation.

♦ Order Processing: Physical distribution assortment is a more involving decision that starts with the customer's order. Customer's order should be accurately and meticulously processed with the main objective of satisfying customer's request. As Kotler, (2005:389) puts it "companies are making great progress in speeding up order handling, that is to computers" the procedure for order sorting include: transmission of order to sales person, order entry and customer credit check; inventory and production schedule, order invoice shipment, and receipt of payment, quick order processing encourage prompt patronage of the firm.

- Warehousing: Warehousing is synonymous with storage management which is concerned with the size, number and location of facilities to house inventory. According to Kotler, (2005:589) "every company has to store its finished goods until they are sold. A storage function is necessary because production and consumption cycles rarely match". An organization must decide on most desirable arrangement to maintain its stocks in warehouse.
- Inventory: Good inventory management is very important to the successful operation of most organizations. Inventory is see by Stevenson, (2002:384) as "a stock of goods that is held for future use". Inventories are classified by the same author to include:
  - Raw materials and purchase parts.
  - Partially completed goods and (work-in-progress).
  - Finished goods and
  - Parts, tools and supplies. Products must be stored in a way that will make up for inaccuracies in demand forecasts. Inventory management as observed as observed by Schewe, (2005) is a way of safe guiding against inability to meet demand directly from the assembly line. It involves and expensive activity, for it involves the costs of storage space handling, and insurance as well as costs associated with product obsolescence. Kotler, (2005) observes that inventory decision making involves knowing when to order and how much to order. As inventory goes down, the management must know at what stock levels to place a new order. The optimal order quantity according to

Mecimore, (2007) could be determined mathematically through the formula:

$$Q^* = \frac{\sqrt{2DS}}{C}$$

Where:

Q^* = Economic order quantity

D = The Annual Volume of sales in units

S = The cost of placing an order (one)

C - The cost of storing one item for a year (inventory carrying cost). Determining the correct quantity of a product to order at a given time is the most fundamental inventory management decision. Transportation: Transportation choices affect product pricing, on-time delivery performance and the condition of the goods when they arrive, all of which affect customer satisfaction. In petroleum industry the choice of physical transportation method called for the price equalization fund by government that has brought the idea of bridging. With the bridging of the products by government and its agencies the price of petroleum products has remained uniform in spite of high cost of delivery, and cost of hiring the vehicles from Eastern part of Nigeria to Northern part of Nigeria (Osagie, 2005). In shipping goods to warehouses, dealers and customers, organizations can choose among the five modes of transportation: rail, air, trucks (roads) waterways, and pipeline, Kotler, (2005).

In case of petroleum products the most outstanding modes of transportation used are pipeline and trucks (roads) for refined products which are our main concern in this study. For better understanding of transportation further explanations are made with respect to:

- Containerization: The use of large standardized easy-to-handle containers in which smaller packages can be loaded for shipping (Schewe, 2005:462).
- Piggyback Service:
- Transportation service in which loaded trucks is taken directly onto rail flatcars; it is the use of rail and trucks.
- Pipelines: The use of pipes to transport ware mainly used for certain products that are mostly liquid. They are the most inexpensive transport mode, but only certain types of products can be transported in this way, (Schewe, 2005; Enyioko and Etim, 2006).
- Fishing Back: Water and trucks transportation service arrangement.
- Train-ship: Water and rail transportation services arrangement
- Air-truck: Air and truck transportation services arrangement
- Contact Carrier is an independent organization selling transportation services to others on contract basis.
- Common carrier: Carrier outfit that provides services between predetermined parts on a

schedule basis and is available to all shippers at standard rates.
- ♦ Distribution Centres: A storage facility that takes orders and delivers products.
- ♦ Private Carrier: A company that owns the goods it transports
- ♦ Exempt Carrier: A company that is exempted from state and federal transportation regulations.

In transportation decisions, organizations consider certain criteria as speed, dependability, availability, capability and cost. A further decision due on transportation arrangement is highlighted by Bowerox et at (2003:59) when they say:

> Transportation decisions must consider the complex trade-offs between various transportation modes and their implications for other distribution elements such as warehousing and inventory. As transportation costs change over time, companies need to reanalyze their options in the search for optimal physical distribution arrangement.

Any organization that aspires to succeed in the turbulent environment must be able to design physical distribution strategy that is of marketing concept oriented.

Channels

- Manufacturer to consumer (most direct)
- Manufacturer to wholesaler to retailer to consumer (traditional)

Marketing Strategies and Strategic Marketing

- Manufacturer to agent to retailer to consumer (current)
- Manufacturer to agent to wholesaler to retailer to consumer
- Manufacturer to agent to customer (ex: AMWAY)

Manufacturers

Reasons for direct selling methods

- Manufacturer wants to demonstrate goods.
- Wholesalers, retailers and agents not actively selling.
- Manufacturer unable to convince wholesalers or retailers to stock product.
- High profit margin added to goods by wholesalers and retailers.
- Middlemen unable to transport.

Reasons for indirect selling methods

- Manufacturer does not have the financial resources to distribute goods.
- Distribution channels already established.
- Manufacturer has no knowledge of efficient distribution.
- Manufacturer wishes to use capital for further production.
- Too many consumers in a large area; difficult to reach.
- Manufacturer does not have a wide assortment of goods to enable efficient marketing.

Wholesalers

Reasons for using wholesalers

- Bear risk of selling goods to retailer or consumer
- Storage space
- Decrease transport costs
- Grant credit to retailers
- Able to sell for the manufacturers
- Give advice to manufacturers
- Break down products into smaller quantities

Reasons for bypassing wholesalers

- Limited storage facilities
- Retailers' preferences
- Wholesaler cannot promote products successfully
- Development of wholesalers' own brands
- Desire for closer market contact
- Position of power
- Cost of wholesalers' services
- Price stabilisation
- Need for rapid distribution
- Make more money

Ways of bypassing wholesalers

- Sales offices or branches
- Mail orders
- Direct sales to retailers
- Travelling agents
- Direct Orders

Agents

- Commission agents work for anyone who needs their services. They do not acquire ownership of goods but receive *del credere* commission.
- Selling agents act on an extended contractual basis, selling all of the products of the manufacturer. They have full authority regarding price and terms of sale.
- Buying agents buy goods on behalf of producers and retailers. They have an expert knowledge of the purchasing function.
- Brokers specialize in the sale of one specific product. They receive a brokerage.
- Factory representatives represent more than one manufacturer. They operate within a specific area and sell related lines of goods but have limited authority regarding price and sales terms.

CHAPTER 2

MARKETING CONCEPTS, STRATEGIC DECISIONS AND CONSUMER BEHAVIOUR / MODELS

Concept / Marketing Concept

A concept is the overall idea or structure of something and marketing is how a product is moved through a channel to reach its target consumer. A marketing concept embraces the philosophy that good marketing strategy always has the needs and wants of the target market in mind. Marketing concepts are formed as creative approaches to the problem of how to get a product needed and desired by a group of consumers to be selected and purchased by this group. The crux of good marketing is being able to communicate the benefits of the products to consumers so that they will choose the product over competitors' offerings.

Awareness of the competition is a crucial consideration when developing a marketing concept for a particular product. For example, two companies could produce canned stew that is very close in price, but if one company communicates its product better in terms of convincing potential purchasers that its brand is the better choice, that product sells better than the competitor's. In order to do that, the marketing concept has to focus on the product's unique selling proposition (USP).

The USP supplies a benefit to the consumer that competing products don't. For instance, a canned stew with sweet potatoes in it rather than regular potatoes could be marketed as more nutritious and flavourful than competing stews. The product now stands out as offering something different and better than other brands. To increase the likelihood that a consumer will try the product, a coupon for the stew could be included in a print ad in a newspaper or magazine.

Although marketing communication is by its nature creative, it should always be strategic and thoughtful as well. Advertising should interest and motivate the target audience, while creating a desire for the product. For instance, some advertising attracts attention, but seconds later, the product itself is forgotten. Good marketing keeps products in the target consumer's mind. Each marketing concept must also fit in with a company's advertising budget.

Creating fresh ideas to keep the brand relevant to the changing needs and desires of the target market is a crucial marketing concept. For example, the popularity of the Internet as a source of information for many consumers has led to the increasing number of companies that feature blogs or website logs about their products.

The marketing concept of building an organization around the profitable satisfaction of customer needs has helped firms to achieve success in high-growth, moderately competitive markets. However, to be successful in markets in which economic growth has levelled and in which there exist many competitors who follow the marketing concept, a well-developed marketing strategy is required. Such a strategy considers a portfolio of products and takes into account the anticipated moves of competitors in the market.

Production Concept: The concept holds that consumers will favour those products that are widely available and low in cost (Says Law).

Product Concept: The concept holds that consumers will favour those products that offer the most quality performance or innovative features.

Selling Concept: The concept holds that consumers, if left alone will ordinarily not buy enough of the organizations products. The organization must therefore undertake an aggressive selling and promotion effort.

Marketing Concept: Holds that the key to achieving organisational goals consists in determining the needs and wants of target market and delivering the desired satisfactions more effectively and efficiently than competitors.

Societal marketing Concept: The concept holds that the organisation task is to determine the needs, wants and interest of target markets and to deliver the desired satisfactions more effectively and efficiently that competitors in a way that preserves or enhances the consumers and the society's well being.

Marketing Oriented Strategic Planning is the managerial process of developing and maintaining a viable fir between the organisation objectives, skills and resources and its changing marketing opportunities.

Strategic Planning

The aim of strategic planning is to shape and reshape the company's business and product so that they yield target profit and growth.

3 Key ideas in defining Strategic Planning

- business as an investment portfolio
- future profit potentials of each business unit
- strategy (game plan)

Figure 2.1: The Strategic Planning, Implementation and Control Process

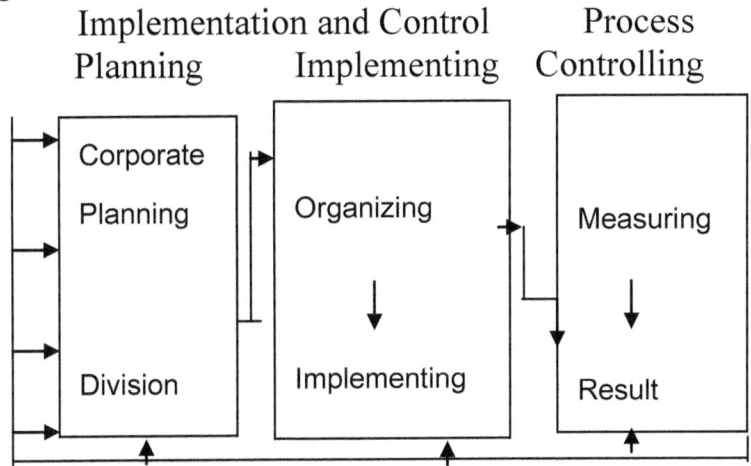

Source: Kotler, P.(1994) Marketing Management: Analysis, Planning Implementation and Control Eight edition. New Jersey: Prentice Hall Inc. P.63

Four major characteristics/factors for High Performance Business are:

(1) Defining the stakeholders :
- Owners/Shareholders
- Employees
- Customers
- Suppliers
- Distributors
- Government

(2) Work processes (Department)

(3) Resources:
-Manager
-Materials
-Finance
-Machines
-Information

(4) Organisation:
-Structure
-Policies
-Culture

Figure 2.2: The Model (Arthur D. Little 1992)

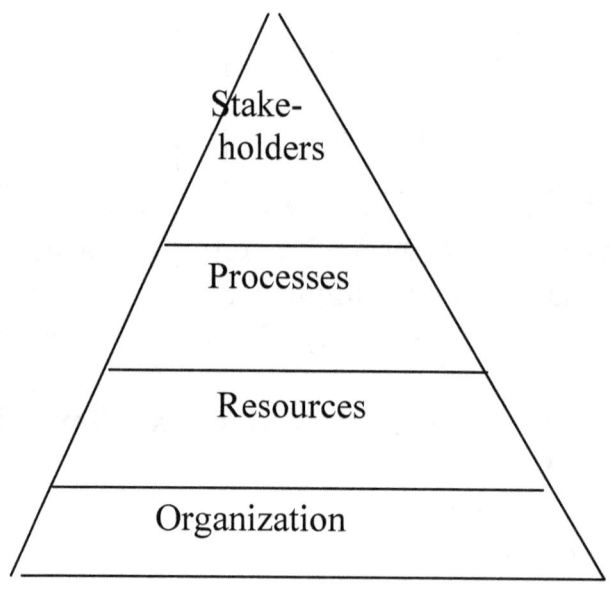

Corporate Strategic Planning

Done at Corporate headquarters; the four major planning activities are:

(1) Defining the corporate mission:-

Marketing Strategies and Strategic Marketing

i. What is our business?

ii Who is our customer?

iii What is value of the customer?

iv What will our business be?

(2) Establishing strategic business units (SBUs)

(3) Assign Resources to each Strategic Business Units (SBU):

(4) Planning new business

Assign Resources to Each Strategic Business Units (SBU):

The purpose of identifying the company's SBUs is to assign to these units strategic planning goals and appropriate funding. These units send their plan to the company headquarters which approves them or send them back for revision. Headquarters reviews these plans in order to decide which of its SBUs to build, maintain, harvest and divest (bmhd).

Boston Consulting Group Model for Portfolio evaluation

Figure 2.3: BCG Model

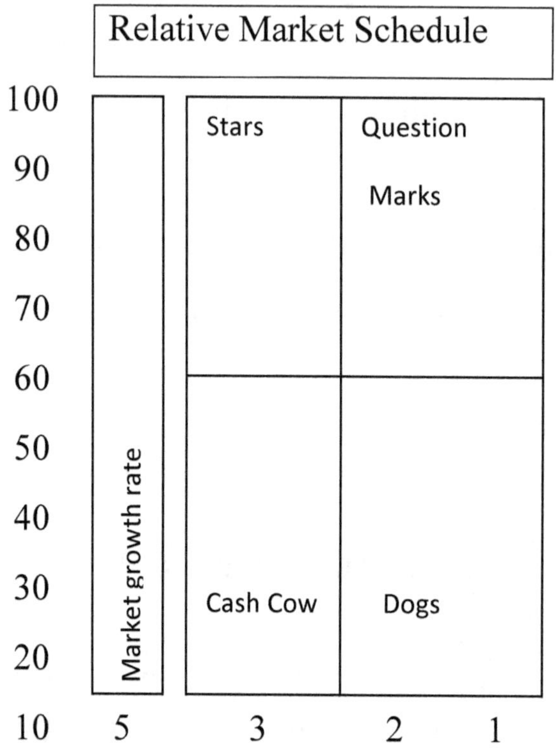

Relative Market Schedule	
Stars	Question Marks
Cash Cow	Dogs

(Market growth rate: 10–100; Relative market share: 5, 3, 2, 1)

QM = business that operate in high growth market but have low relative market share.

Stars = QM becomes successful if it becomes star that is high market growth rate and high relative market shares. Star produces positive cash flow for the firm.

Cash Cow = Low market growth rate with relative market share, it needs milking.

Dogs = Weak market shares and low growth rate, they typically generate low profit.

Consumer Behaviour

Consumer Buying Behavior refers to the buying behavior of the ultimate consumer. A firm needs to analyze buying behavior for:

- Buyers reactions to a firms marketing strategy has a great impact on the firm's success.
- The marketing concept stresses that a firm should create a marketing mix (MM) that satisfies (gives utility to) customers, therefore need to analyze the what, where, when and how consumers buy.
- Marketers can better predict how consumers will respond to marketing strategies.

Stages of the Consumer Buying Process

Six Stages to the Consumer Buying Decision Process (For complex decisions). Actual purchasing is only one stage of the process. Not all decision processes lead to a purchase. All consumer decisions do not always include all 6 stages, determined by the degree of complexity. The 6 stages are:

1. *Problem Recognition*(awareness of need)-- difference between the desired state and the actual condition. Deficit in assortment of products. Hunger--Food. Hunger stimulates your need to eat. Can be stimulated by the marketer through product information--did not know you were deficient?

I.E., see a commercial for a new pair of shoes, stimulates your recognition that you need a new pair of shoes.
2. *Information search--*
    - Internal search, memory.
    - External search if you need more information. Friends and relatives (word of mouth). Marketer dominated sources; comparison shopping; public sources etc.

    A successful information search leaves a buyer with possible alternatives, the *evoked set*.

    Hungry, want to go out and eat, evoked set is

    - Chinese food
    - African food
    - Burger king
    - *Edearo*
    - *Achara Mirii Ngwa*
    - *Ugba*
    - Tapioca etc.
3. *Evaluation of Alternatives--*need to establish criteria for evaluation, features the buyer wants or does not want. Rank/weight alternatives or resume search. May decide that you want to eat something spicy, African gets highest rank etc. If not satisfied with your choice then return to the search phase. Can you think of another restaurant? Look in the yellow pages etc. Information from different sources may be treated differently. Marketers try to influence by "framing" alternatives.

Marketing Strategies and Strategic Marketing

4. *Purchase decision*--Choose buying alternative, includes product, package, store, method of purchase etc.
5. *Purchase*--May differ from decision, time lapse between 4 & 5, product availability.
6. *Post-Purchase Evaluation*--outcome: Satisfaction or Dissatisfaction. *Cognitive Dissonance*, have you made the right decision. This can be reduced by warranties, after sales communication etc. After eating an African meal, may think that really you wanted a Chinese meal instead.

Figure 2.4: Model of Buyer Behavior

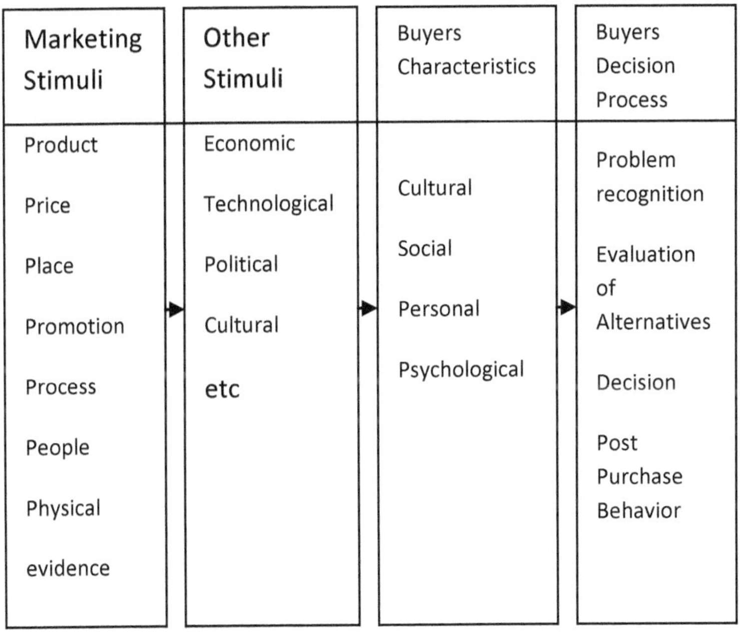

Marketing Stimuli	Other Stimuli	Buyers Characteristics	Buyers Decision Process
Product	Economic		Problem recognition
Price	Technological	Cultural	
Place	Political	Social	Evaluation of Alternatives
Promotion	Cultural	Personal	
Process	etc	Psychological	Decision
People			Post Purchase Behavior
Physical evidence			

Figure 2.5: Maslow's Hierarchy of Needs

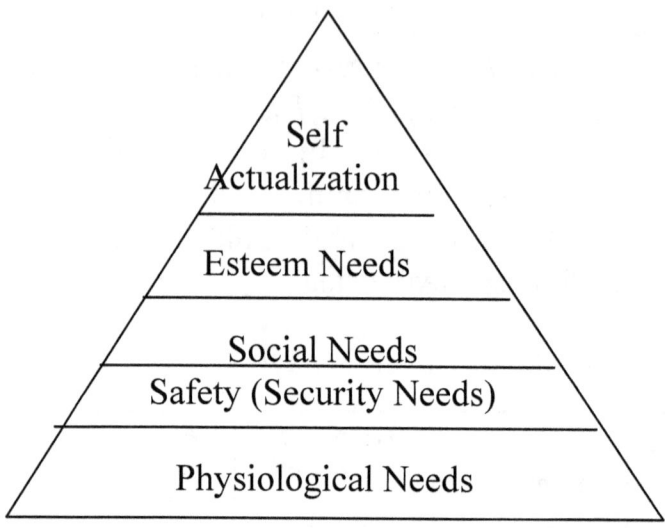

Figure 2.6: Detailed Model Factors Influencing Behaviour

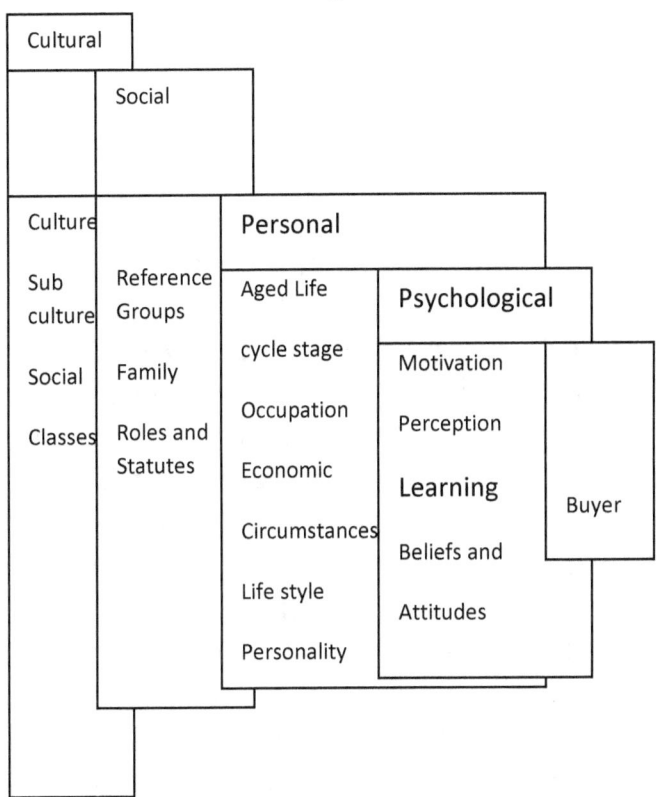

Buying Decision Process

Buying Roles

        Initiator   –   1st who first suggests
        Influencer -   Person who influences the purchase decision
        Decider   -   Person who decides
        Buyer   -   Who buys
        User   -   Uses

Types of Buying Decision
1. Complex buying behaviour
2. Dissonance – reducing buying behavior
3. Habitual buying behavior
4. Variety – seeking buying behavior

The Use of Herd Behaviour in Marketing.

In an article entitled "Swarming the shelves: How shops can exploit people's herd mentality to increase sales", *The Economist* recently reported a recent conference in Rome on the subject of the simulation of adaptive human behaviour. Mechanisms to increase impulse buying and get people "to buy more by playing on the herd instinct" were shared. The basic idea is that people will buy more of products that are seen to be popular, and several feedback mechanisms to get product popularity information to consumers are mentioned, including smart-cart technology and the use of Radio Frequency Identification Tag technology. A "swarm-moves" model was introduced by a Princeton researcher, which is appealing to supermarkets because it can "increase sales without the need to give people discounts." Large retailers Wal-Mart in the United States, and Tesco in Britain plan to test the technology in spring 2007.

Other recent studies on the "power of social influence" include an "artificial music market in which some 14,000 people downloaded previously unknown songs" (Columbia University, New York); a Japanese chain of convenience stores which orders its products based on "sales data from department stores and research companies;" a Massachusetts company exploiting knowledge of social networking to improve sales; and online retailers who are increasingly informing consumers about "which products are popular with like-minded consumers" (e.g., Amazon, eBay).

Customer Focus

Many companies today have a customer focus (or customer orientation). This implies that the company focuses its activities and products on consumer demands. Generally there are three ways of doing this: the customer-driven approach, the sense of identifying market changes and the product innovation approach.

In the consumer-driven approach, consumer wants are the drivers of all strategic marketing decisions. No strategy is pursued until it passes the test of consumer research. Every aspect of a market offering, including the nature of the product itself, is driven by the needs of potential consumers. The starting point is always the consumer. The rationale for this approach is that there is no point spending R&D funds developing products that people will not buy. History attests to many products that were commercial failures in spite of being technological breakthroughs.

A formal approach to this customer-focused marketing is known as SIVA (Brown, 1998) (Solution, Information, Value, Access). This system is basically the four Ps renamed and reworded to provide a customer focus. The SIVA Model provides a demand/customer centric version alternative to the well-known 4Ps supply side model (product, price, place, promotion) of marketing management.

Product	->	Solution
Promotion	->	Information
Price	->	Value
Place	->	Access

The four elements of the SIVA model are:

1. Solution: How appropriate is the solution to the customers problem/need?
2. Information: Does the customer know about the solution, and if so how, who from, do they know enough to let them make a buying decision?
3. Value: Does the customer know the value of the transaction, what it will cost, what are the benefits, what might they have to sacrifice, what will be their reward?
4. Access: Where can the customer find the solution? How easily/locally/remotely can they buy it and take delivery?

This model was proposed by Chekitan Dev and Don Schultz in the Marketing Management Journal of the American Marketing Association, and presented by them in Market Leader - the journal of the Marketing Society in the UK. The model focuses heavily on the customer and how they view the transaction.

Measuring and Forecasting Market Demand

Market demand for a product is the total that would be brought by a defined customer group in a defined geographical area in a defined time period in a defined marketing environment under a defined marketing programmeme.

Market Forecast – Only one level of industry marketing experience will actually occur. The market do corresponding to this level is called market forecast.

Market Potential is the limit approached by market demand as industry marketing experiences approach infinity for a given environment.

Company Demand: Company Demand is the company's share of market demand ie $Q_1 = SiQ$

Where; Q_1 = Company's Demand

S_1 = Company's Market share

Q = Total Market Demand

Company Sales Forecast – the expected level of company sales based on a closer marketing plan and an assured marketing environment.

Sales Quota: Sales goal set for a product line, Company division or sales representative. It is primarily a managerial device for defining and stimulating sales effort.

Sales Budget: Is a conservative estimate of the expected

income of sales and is used primarily for making continuous purchasing, production and cash flow decision.

Company's Sales Potential: Is the limit approached by company demand as company marketing effort increases relative to competitors

Estimating Current Demand: Total market potential is the maximum amount of sales that might be available to all the firms in an industry during a given period under a given level of industry marketing effort and environmental conditions.

$Q = nqp$ " where:

Q = total market potential

n = No of buyers in the specific period/market under the given assumptions.

q = quality purchased by an average buyer.

P = price of an average unit of product.

Forecasting Methods

1. Survey buyers intention/opinion
2. Composite of sales opinion
3. Expert opinion
4. Market test method
5. The series analysis (component
   Q = Quantity of past sales

   T = Trend

   C = Cycle

Marketing Strategies and Strategic Marketing

S = Season

E = Erratic event

$Qt + 1 = \alpha Qt + (1-\alpha)Qt$

Where $Qt + 1$ = sales forecast for next period

α= The smoothing constraint , where $0 \leq \& \leq 1$

Qt = current sales in period t

Qt = smoothed sales in period t.

Suppose the smoothing constant is 0.4, current sales = N50, 000 and smoothed sales are N40, 000, the sales forecast is Qt -1 = 0.4 (N50,000) + 0.6 (N40,000) = 44,000

CHAPTER 3

MARKETING INFORMATION SYSTEM AND MARKETING RESEARCH

Marketing Information System (MIS) is a set of procedures and methods designed to generate, analyze, disseminate, and store anticipated marketing decision information on a regular, continuous basis. An information system can be used operationally, managerially, and strategically for several aspects of marketing.

We all know that no marketing activity can be carried out in isolation, when we say it doesn't work in isolation that means there are various forces - external or internal, controllable or uncontrollable which are working on it. Thus to know which forces are acting on it and its impact, the marketer needs to gather the data through the company's own resources which in terms of marketing we can say he is trying to gather the market information or form a *Marketing Information System*. This collection of information is a continuous process that gathers data from a variety of sources synthesizes it and sends it to those responsible for meeting the market places needs. The effectiveness of marketing decision is proved if it has a strong information system offering the firm a Competitive advantage. Marketing Information should not be approached in an infrequent manner. If research is done this way, a firm could face these risks:

1. Opportunities may be missed.

2. There may be a lack of awareness of environmental changes and competitors' actions.
3. Data collection may be difficult to analyze over several time periods.
4. Marketing plans and decisions may not be properly reviewed.
5. Data collection may be disjointed.
6. Previous studies may not be stored in an easy to use format.
7. Time lags may result if a new study is required.
8. Actions may be reactionary rather than anticipatory.

The total information needs of the marketing department can be specified and satisfied via a marketing intelligence network, which contains three components:

1. Continuous monitoring is the procedure by which the changing environment is regularly viewed.
2. Marketing research is used to obtain information on particular marketing issues.
3. Data warehousing involves the retention of all types of relevant company records, as well as the information collected through continuous monitoring and marketing research that is kept by the organization.

Depending on a firm's resources and the complexity of its needs, a marketing intelligence network may or may not be fully computerized. The ingredients for a good MIS are consistency, completeness, and orderliness. Marketing plans should be implemented on the basis of information obtained from the intelligence network.

An Marketing Information System offers many advantages:
1. Organized data collection.

2. A broad perspective.
3. The storage of important data.
4. An avoidance of crises.
5. Coordinated marketing plans.
6. Speed in obtaining sufficient information to make decisions.
7. Data amassed and kept over several time periods.
8. The ability to do a cost-benefit analysis.

The disadvantages of a Marketing information system are high initial time and labour costs and the complexity of setting up an information system. Marketers often complain that they lack enough marketing information or the right kind, or have too much of the wrong kind. The solution is an effective

Marketing Information System

The information needed by marketing managers comes from three main sources:

1) Internal company information – E.g. sales, orders, customer profiles, stocks, customer service reports etc
2) Marketing intelligence – This can be information gathered from many sources, including suppliers, customers, and distributors. Marketing intelligence is a catchall term to include all the everyday information about developments in the market that helps a business prepare and adjust its marketing plans. It is possible to buy intelligence information from outside suppliers (e.g. IDC, ORG, MARG) who set up data gathering systems to support commercial intelligence products that can be profitably sold to all players in a market.
(3) Market research – Management cannot always wait for information to arrive in bits and pieces from internal sources. Also, sources of market intelligence cannot

always be relied upon to provide relevant or up-to-date information (particularly for smaller or niche market segments). In such circumstances, businesses often need to undertake specific studies to support their marketing strategy – this is market research. Marketing Information Systems consist of people, equipment and procedures together with the functions of sorting, analysing, evaluating and distribution needed for accurate information to achieve marketing decisions timely.

Figure 3.1: Development Information

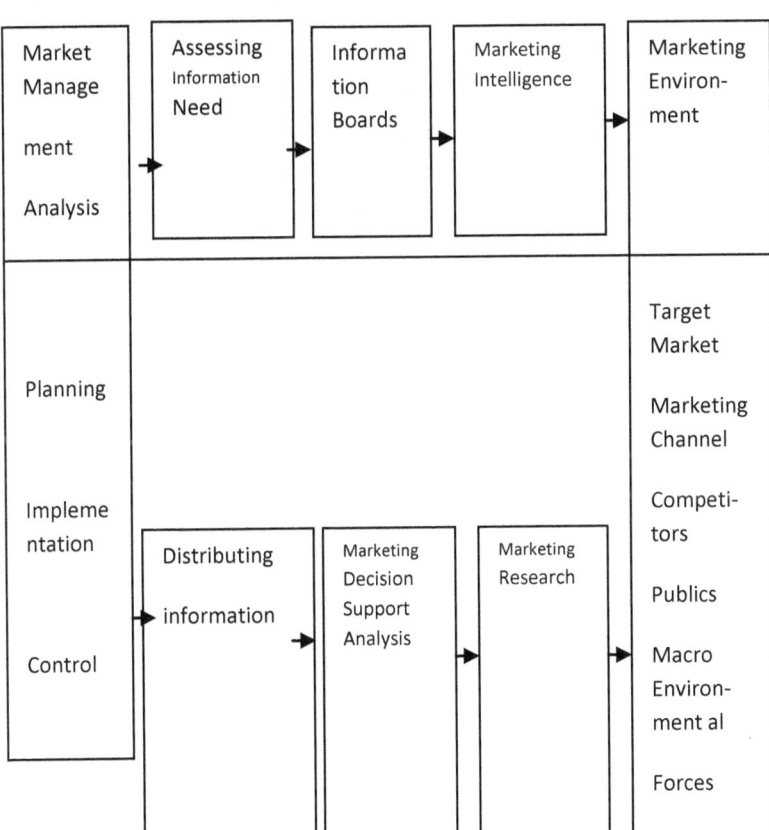

The Value of Information

Information can be useful, but what determines its real value to the organization? In general, the value of information is determined by:

- The ability and willingness to act on the information.
- The accuracy of the information.
- The level of indecisiveness that would exist without the information.
- The amount of variation in the possible results.
- The level of risk aversion.
- The reaction of competitors to any decision improved by the information.
- The cost of the information in terms of time and money.

Marketing Strategies and Strategic Marketing

Table 3.1: Marketing Research Activities

Type of Research

- **A. Business/Economic Corporate Research**
  1. Industry/Market Characteristics and Needs — 83
  2. Acquisition and Diversification studies — 53
  3. Market share analysis — 79
  4. Internal employee studies — 54
- **B. Pricing**
  5. Cost Analysis — 60
  6. Profit Analysis — 59
  7. Prices Elasticity — 45
  8. Demand Analysis — 57
     (a) Market Potential — 74
     (b) Sales — 69
     (c) Sales Forecast — 67
  9. Comparative Pricing Analysis — 63
- **C. Product**
  10. Concept of Development and Testing — 68
  11. Brand name generation and testing — 38
  12. Test Market — 45
  13. Product testing of existing market — 47
  14. Packing Design Studies — 31
  15. Competitive Product studies — 58
- **D. Distribution**
  16. Plant/Warehouse Location studies — 23
  17. Channel performance studies — 29
  18. Channel Coverage studies — 26
  19. Export/International studies — 19
- **E. Promotion**
  20. Motivation research — 37
  21. Media research — 57
  22. Copy research — 50

	23. Advertising effectiveness	65
	24. Competitive advertising studies	47
	25. Public image studies	60
	26. Sales force compensation studies	30
	27. Sales force quota studies	26
	28. Sales force territory structure	31
	29. Premiums, Coupons and deals studies	36
E.	**Buying Behaviour**	
	30. Brand preference	54
	31. Brand attitudes	53
	32. Product satisfaction	68
	33. Purchase behavior	61
	34. Purchase intentions	60
	35. Brand awareness	59
	36. Segmentation studies	60

Marketing Research for Strategic Decision Making

The two most common uses of marketing research are for diagnostic analysis to understand the market and the firm's current performance, and opportunity analysis to define any unexploited opportunities for growth. Marketing research studies include consumer studies, distribution studies, semantic scaling, multidimensional scaling, intelligence studies, projections, and conjoint analysis. A few of these are explained below:

- Semantic scaling: a very simple rating of how consumers perceive the physical attributes of a product, and what the ideal values of those attributes would be. Semantic scaling is not very accurate since the consumers are polled according to an ordinal ranking so mathematical averaging is

not possible. For example, 8 is not necessarily twice as much as 4 in an ordinal ranking system. Furthermore, each person uses the scale differently.
- Multidimensional scaling (MDS) addresses the problems associated with semantic scaling by polling the consumer for pair-wise comparisons between products or between one product and the ideal. The assumption is that while people cannot report reliably which attributes drive their choices, they can report perceptions of similarities between brands. However, MDS analyses do not indicate the relative importance between attributes.
- Conjoint analysis infers the relative importance of attributes by presenting consumers with a set of features of two hypothetical products and asking them which product they prefer. This question is repeated over several sets of attribute values. The results allow one to predict which attributes are the more important, the combination of attribute values that is the most preferred. From this information, the expected market share of a given design can be estimated.

Marketing Research

Managers need information in order to introduce products and services that create value in the mind of the customer. But the perception of value is a subjective one, and what customers value this year may be quite different from what they value next year. As such, the attributes that create value cannot simply be deduced from common knowledge. Rather, data must be collected and analyzed. The goal of marketing research is to provide the facts and direction that managers need to make their more important marketing decisions.

To maximize the benefit of marketing research, those who use it need to understand the research process and its limitations.

Figure 3.2: Marketing Research Process

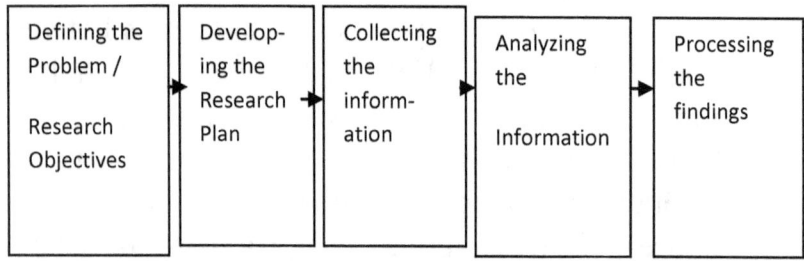

Kinear, T.C, and Root, A.R. (1989) Survey of Marketing Organisation, Functions, Budget and Compensation.

Marketing Research vs. Market Research

These terms often are used interchangeably, but technically there is a difference.

Market research deals specifically with the gathering of information about a market's size and trends. *Marketing research* covers a wider range of activities. While it may involve market research, marketing research is a more general systematic process that can be applied to a variety of marketing problems.

The Role And Limitations of Marketing Research

Marketing research serves marketing management by providing information which is relevant to decision making. Marketing research does not itself make the decisions, nor does it guarantee success. Rather, marketing research helps to reduce the uncertainty surrounding the decisions to be made. In order to do so effectively, marketing research has to be systematic, objective and analytical.

The manager or other individual initiating the research must provide guidance to the researcher in the form of a research brief. This document should state the purpose of the research, its objectives, the time by which it must be completed, the budget to which the researcher must work in developing the research design and the timing and frequency of any interim reports which the researcher is expected to make. Having read, questioned and understood the research brief the onus is then upon the marketing researcher to respond by preparing the research design. Research design begins with an accurate and, as far as is possible, precise definition of the problem. This is followed by the generation of hypotheses. There will then be an intermediate stage whereby the hypotheses are restated in a testable form, i.e. the null form. This will probably only be done if it is intended that statistical analysis is to be undertaken. Where the research is more qualitative in nature then it is still recommended that hypotheses should be developed. These should include alternative hypotheses; depending upon what is already known about the research problem

one of three types of study might be undertaken, i.e. an exploratory study, a descriptive study or a causal study. Before proceeding further, the researcher has to develop an analysis plan. It is only when the analysis plan has been considered that fieldwork, in the form of data collection, should be undertaken. The final step in the research design would be to write the report. Customer oriented marketing researchers will have noted from the outset of the research which topics and issues are of particular importance to the person(s) who initiated the research and will weigh the content of their reports accordingly. Marketing researchers work with probabilistic models of the form:
$y = f(x_1)..(fx_2)...f(x_n)...$

This reflects the fact that in order for a target market share to be reached some promotion (amount unknown) is **necessary** but will not be **sufficient,** on its own, to achieve the target. Y is a function of a number of variables and the interactions between them. The model is further complicated by the fact that these interactions are themselves often not understood. It is for these reasons that marketing researchers cannot guarantee that decisions based on their information will always prove 'successful'. Rather the best that a competent researcher and a well designed study will be able to offer is a reduction in the amount of uncertainty surrounding the decision.

Here is a case to be considered. A small engineering firm had purchased a prototype tree-lifter from a private research company. This machine was suitable for lifting semi-mature trees, complete with root-ball intact, and transplanting such trees in another location. It was thought to have potential in certain types of tree nurseries and plantations.

The problem with the objective is that the marketing manager needs to know the potential market for the new tree-lifter is that it is not attainable. One could find out how many tree-lifters were currently being sold but this is not the same as the objective set by the marketing manager. The market potential for any new brand is a function of at least 4 things, as shown in Figure 3.3.

Figure 3.3: The Components of Market Potential

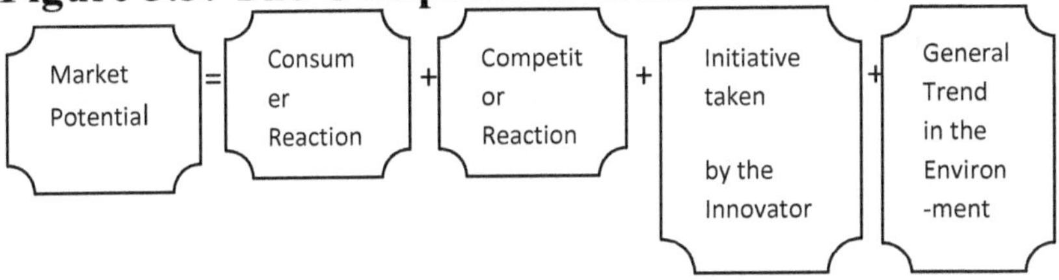

Market Potential = Consumer Reaction + Competitor Reaction + Initiative taken by the Innovator + General Trend in the Environment

It was possible to test customer reaction to the concept of the new tree-lifter by showing pictures, line drawings and by supplying product specifications to prospective buyers. However, since the company had not decided their pricing policy an important element could not be tested. In large measure, it was also possible to gauge the likely reaction from competitors. The researchers began by looking at the basis of competition to determine whether it was on price, product quality or unique product features.

The researchers were able to look at precedents. They examined the pattern of response on past occasions when one or other of those companies already in the market had launched a new product. An audit of the environment was undertaken too, but the missing component was the company's' own plans for exploiting the market. Since the company had no involvement in the agricultural engineering sector, prior to acquiring the rights to the tree-lifter, they had no agreements with distributors, no idea of which, if any, of the distributors would be prepared to stock their product; they had no salesmen trained in selling into this industry and so on. The product's potential depended very much on such initiatives.

The solution would have been to undertake a study which would have described the market in detail in terms of customers, competitors and the environment. The company could then have put a marketing plan together and conducted a follow-up study to test their propositions out on the marketplace.

The Marketing Research Process

Once the need for marketing research has been established, most marketing research projects involve these steps:

1. Define the problem
2. Determine research design
3. Identify data types and sources
4. Design data collection forms and questionnaire
5. Determine sample plan and size
6. Collect the data
7. Analyze and interpret the data
8. Prepare the research report

Problem Definition

The decision problem faced by management must be translated into a market research problem in the form of questions that define the information that is required to make the decision and how this information can be obtained. Thus, the decision problem is translated into a research problem. For example, a decision problem may be whether to launch a new product. The corresponding research problem might be to assess whether the market would accept the new product.

The objective of the research should be defined clearly. To ensure that the true decision problem is addressed, it is useful for the researcher to outline possible scenarios of the research results and then for the decision maker to formulate plans of action under each scenario. The use of such scenarios can ensure that the purpose of the research is agreed upon before it commences.

Research Design

Marketing research can be classified in one of three categories:

- Exploratory research
- Descriptive research
- Causal research

These classifications are made according to the objective of the research. In some cases the research will fall into one of these categories, but in other cases different phases of the same research project will fall into different categories.

- *Exploratory research* has the goal of formulating problems more precisely, clarifying concepts, gathering explanations, gaining insight, eliminating impractical ideas, and forming hypotheses. Exploratory research can be performed using a literature search, surveying certain people about their experiences, focus groups, and case studies. When surveying people, exploratory research studies would not try to acquire a representative sample, but rather, seek to interview those who are knowledgeable and who might be able to provide insight concerning the relationship among variables. Case studies can include contrasting situations or benchmarking against an organization known for its excellence. Exploratory research may develop hypotheses, but it does not seek to test them. Exploratory research is characterized by its flexibility.
- *Descriptive research* is more rigid than exploratory research and seeks to describe users of a product, determine the proportion of the population that uses a product, or predict future demand for a product. As opposed to exploratory research, descriptive research should define questions, people surveyed, and the method of analysis prior to beginning data collection. In other words, the who, what, where, when, why, and how aspects of the research should be defined. Such preparation allows one the opportunity to make any required

changes before the costly process of data collection has begun.

There are two basic types of descriptive research: longitudinal studies and cross-sectional studies. Longitudinal studies are time series analyses that make repeated measurements of the same individuals, thus allowing one to monitor behaviour such as brand-switching. However, longitudinal studies are not necessarily representative since many people may refuse to participate because of the commitment required. Cross-sectional studies sample the population to make measurements at a specific point in time. A special type of cross-sectional analysis is a cohort analysis, which tracks an aggregate of individuals who experience the same event within the same time interval over time. Cohort analyses are useful for long-term forecasting of product demand.

- *Causal research* seeks to find cause and effect relationships between variables. It accomplishes this goal through laboratory and field experiments. Causal research deals with the "why" questions. That is, there are occasions when the researcher will want to know why a change in one variable brings about a change in another. If he/she can understand the causes of the effects observed then our ability to predict and control such events is increased.

Fig. 3.4: The Research Design

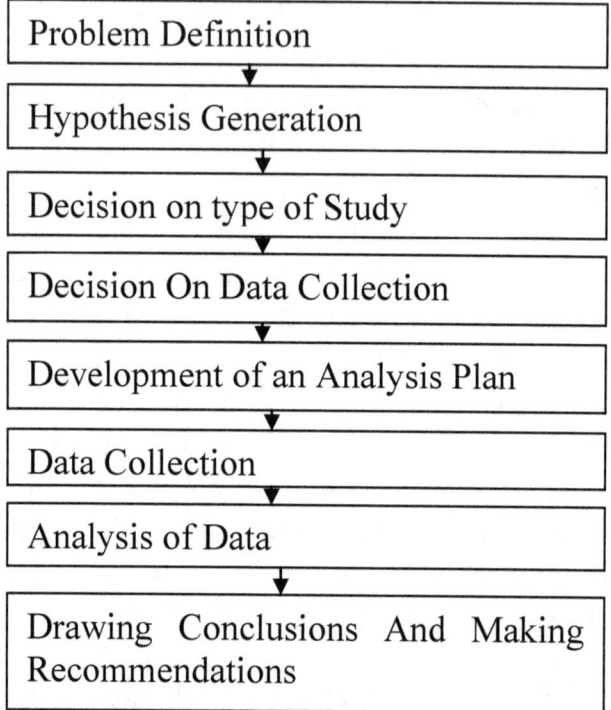

Step 1: Problem Definition
The point has already been made that the decision-maker should clearly communicate the purpose of the research to the marketing researcher but it is often the case that the objectives are not fully explained to the individual carrying out the study. In situations, in which the researcher senses that the decision-maker is either unwilling or unable to fully articulate the objectives then he/she will have to pursue an indirect line of questioning. One approach is to take the problem statement supplied by the decision-maker and to break this down into key

components and/or terms and to explore these with the decision-maker. For example, the decision-maker could be asked what he has in mind when he uses the term market potential. This is a legitimate question since the researcher is charged with the responsibility to develop a research design which will provide the right kind of information. Another approach is to focus the discussions with the person commissioning the research on the decisions which would be made given alternative findings which the study might come up with. This process frequently proves of great value to the decision-maker in that it helps him think through the objectives and perhaps select the most important of the objectives.

Other helpful procedures include brainstorming, reviews of research on related problems and researching secondary sources of information as well as studying competitive products. Kerlinger, (1994) suggests that a well-defined marketing research problem tends to have three common characteristics as shown in figure 3.5.

Figure 3.5: Characteristics of a sound definition of the research problem

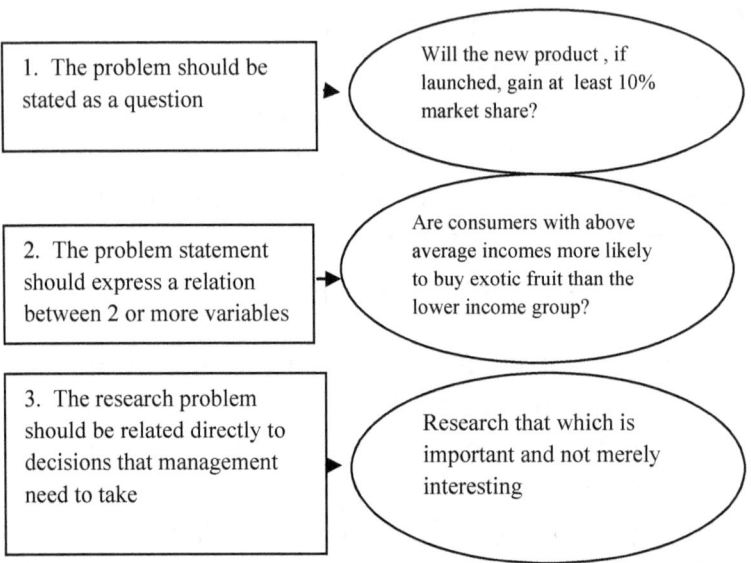

Step 2: Hypothesis Generation

A hypothesis is a conjectural statement regarding the relation between two or more variables. There are two key characteristics which all hypotheses must have: they must be statements of the relationship between variables and they must carry clear implications for testing the stated relations. These characteristics imply that it is relationships, rather than variables, which are tested; the hypotheses specify how the variables are related and that these are measurable or potentially measurable. Statements lacking any or all of these characteristics are not research hypotheses. For example, consider the following hypothesis: "There is no relationship between a farmer's educational level and his degree of innovativeness with respect to new farming technologies."

Hypotheses are central to progress in research. They will direct the researcher's efforts by forcing him/her to concentrate on gathering the facts which will enable the hypotheses to be tested. The point has been made that it is all too easy when conducting research to collect "interesting data" as opposed to "important data". Data and questions which enable researchers to test explicit hypotheses are important. The rest are merely interesting.

There is a second advantage of stating hypotheses, namely that implicit notions or explanations for events become explicit and this often leads to modifications of these explanations, even before data is collected.

On occasion a given hypotheses may be too broad to be tested. However, other testable hypotheses may be deduced from it. A problem really cannot be solved unless it is reduced to hypothesis form, because a problem is a question, usually of a broad nature, and is not directly testable.

Step 3: Decision on type of study

Marketing research can be carried out on one of three levels: exploratory, descriptive or causal.

Fig: 3.6: Three Types of Marketing Research

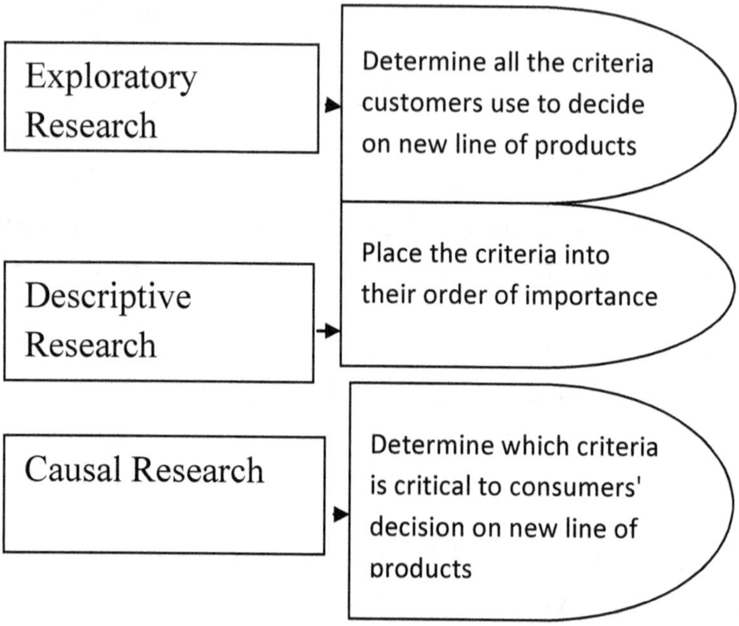

Research Type	Purpose
Exploratory Research	Determine all the criteria customers use to decide on new line of products
Descriptive Research	Place the criteria into their order of importance
Causal Research	Determine which criteria is critical to consumers' decision on new line of products

Step 4: Decision On Data Collection Method

The next set of decisions concerns the method(s) of data gathering to be employed. The main methods of data collection are secondary data searches, observation, the survey, experimentation and consumer panels. Each of these topics is dealt with later on, so they are simply noted here.

Fig. 3.7: Data Collection Methods

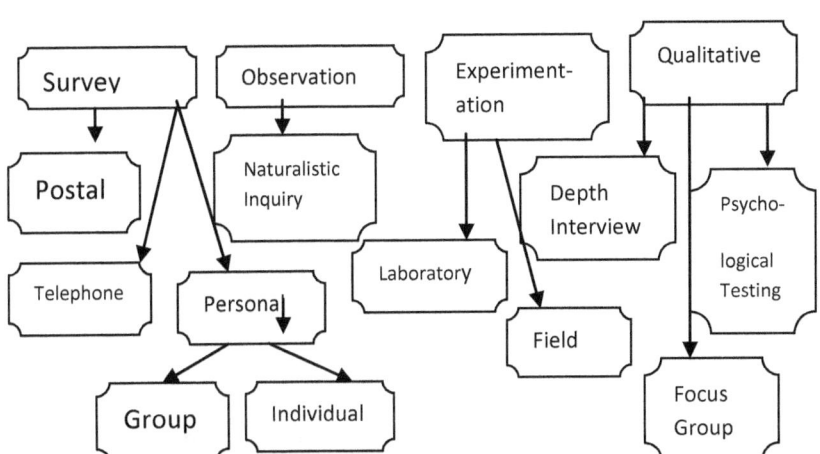

Step 5: Development of an Analysis Plan: Those new to marketing research often intuitively believe that decisions about the techniques of analysis to be used can be left until after the data has been collected. Such an approach is ill-advised. Before interviews are conducted the following checklist should be applied:

Is it known how each and every question is to be analysed? (e.g. which univariate or bivariate descriptive statistics, tests of association, parametric or nonparametric hypotheses tests, or multivariate methods are to be used?)

· Does the researcher have a sufficiently sound grasp of these techniques to apply them with confidence and to explain them to the decision-maker who commissioned the study?

· Does the researcher have the means to perform these

calculations? (e.g. access to a computer which has an analysis programme which he/she is familiar with? Or, if the calculations have to be performed manually, is there sufficient time to complete them and then to check them?)

· If a computer programme is to be used at the data analysis stage, have the questions been properly coded?

· Have the questions been scaled correctly for the chosen statistical technique? (e.g. a t-test cannot be used on data which is only ranked)

There is little point in spending time and money on collecting data which subsequently is not or cannot be analysed. Therefore consideration has to be given to issues such as these before the fieldwork is undertaken.

Step 6: Data Collection

At this stage the researcher is ready to go into the field and collect data. The various issues relating to data collection constitute the main body of the text and therefore, are not dwelt upon here.

Step 7: Analysis of Data

The word 'analysis' has two component parts, the prefix 'ana' meaning 'above' and the Greek root 'lysis' meaning 'to break up or dissolve'. Thus data analysis can be described as: "...a process of resolving data into its constituent components, to reveal its characteristic elements and structure." Where the data is quantitative there are three determinants of the appropriate statistical tools for the purposes of analysis. These are the number of samples to be compared, whether the samples being compared are independent of one another and the level of data measurement.

Suppose a fruit juice processor wishes to test the acceptability of a new drink based on a novel combination of tropical fruit juices. There are several alternative research designs which might be employed, each involving different numbers of samples.

Test A — Comparing sales in a test market and the market share of the product it is targeted to replace. Number of samples = 1

Test B — Comparing the responses of a sample of regular drinkers of fruit juices to those of a sample of non-fruit juice drinkers to a trial formulation. Number of samples = 2

Test C — Comparing the responses of samples of heavy, moderate and infrequent fruit juice drinkers to a trial formulation. Number of samples = 3

The next consideration is whether the samples being compared are dependent (i.e. related) or independent of one another (i.e. unrelated). Samples are said to be dependent, or related, when the measurement taken from one sample in no way affects the measurement taken from another sample. Take for example the outline of test B above. The measurement of the responses of fruit juice drinkers to the trial formulation in no way affects or influences the responses of the sample of non-fruit juice drinkers. Therefore, the samples are independent of one another. Suppose however a sample were given two formulations of fruit juice to taste. That is, the same individuals are asked first to taste formulation X and then to taste formulation Y. The researcher would have two sets of sample results, i.e. responses to product X and responses to product Y. In this case, the samples would be considered dependent or related to one another. This is because the individual will make a comparison of the two products and his/her response to one formulation is likely to affect his/her reaction or evaluation of the other product.

The third factor to be considered is the levels of measurement of the data being used. Data can be nominal, ordinal, interval or ratio scaled. Choosing format (a) would give rise to nominal (or categorical) data and format (b) would yield ratio scaled data. These are at opposite ends of the hierarchy of levels of measurement. If by accident or design format (a) were chosen then the analyst would have only a very small set of statistical tests that could be applied and these are not very powerful in the sense that they are limited to showing association between variables and could not be used to establish cause-and-effect. Format (b), on the other hand, since it gives the analyst ratio data, allows all statistical tests to be used including the more powerful parametric tests whereby cause-and-effect can be established, where it exists. Thus a simple change in the wording of a question can have a fundamental effect upon the nature of the data generated. Figure 3.8 provides a useful guide to making that final selection.

Marketing Strategies and Strategic Marketing

Fig. 3.8: Selecting Statistical Tests

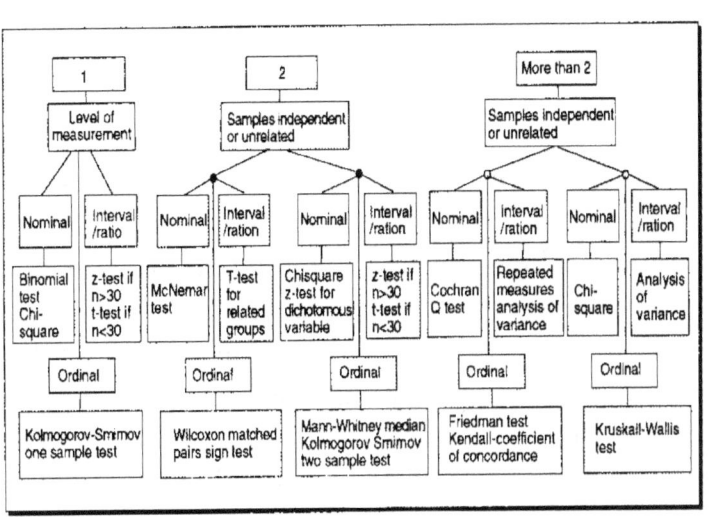

The individual responsible for commissioning the research may be unfamiliar with the technicalities of statistical tests but he/she should at least be aware that the number of samples, their dependence or independence and the levels of measurement does affect how the data can be analysed. Those who submit marketing research proposals involving quantitative data should demonstrate an awareness of the factors that determine the mode of analysis and a capability to undertake such analysis.

Marketing researchers have to plan ahead for the analysis stage. It often happens that data processing begins whilst the data gathering is still underway. Whether the data is to be analysed manually or through the use of a computer programme, data can be coded, cleaned (i.e. errors removed) and the proposed analytical tests tried out to ensure that they are effective before all of the data has been collected.

Step 8: Drawing Conclusions And Making Recommendations

The final part of the research is devoted to the topic of report writing. However, it is perhaps worth noting that the end products of marketing research are conclusions and recommendations. With respect to the marketing planning function, marketing research helps to identify potential threats and opportunities, generates alternative courses of action, provides information to enable marketing managers to evaluate those alternatives and advises on the implementation of the alternatives.

Too often marketing research reports chiefly comprise a lengthy series of tables of statistics accompanied by a few brief comments which verbally describe what is already self-evident from the tables. Without interpretation, data remains of potential, as opposed to actual use. When conclusions are drawn from raw data and when recommendations are made then data is converted into information. It is information which management needs to reduce the inherent risks and uncertainties in management decision making.

Customer oriented marketing researchers will have noted from the outset of the research which topics and issues are of particular importance to the person(s) who initiated the research and will weigh the content of their reports accordingly. That is, the researcher should determine what the marketing manager's priorities are with respect to the research study.

Data Types and Sources
Secondary Data

Before going through the time and expense of collecting primary data, one should check for secondary data that previously may have been collected for other purposes but that can be used in the immediate study. Secondary data may be internal to the firm, such as sales invoices and warranty cards, or may be external to the firm such as published data or commercially available data. The government census is a valuable source of secondary data.

Secondary data has the advantage of saving time and reducing data gathering costs. The disadvantages are that the data may not fit the problem perfectly and that the accuracy may be more difficult to verify for secondary data than for primary data.

Some secondary data is republished by organizations other than the original source. Because errors can occur and important explanations may be missing in republished data, one should obtain secondary data directly from its source. One also should consider who the source is and whether the results may be biased. There are several criteria that one should use to evaluate secondary data.
- Whether the data is useful in the research study.

- How current the data is and whether it applies to time period of interest.
- Errors and accuracy - whether the data is dependable and can be verified.
- Presence of bias in the data.
- Specifications and methodologies used, including data collection method, response rate, quality and analysis of the data, sample size and sampling technique, and questionnaire design.
- Objective of the original data collection.
- Nature of the data, including definition of variables, units of measure, categories used, and relationships examined.

Primary Data

Often, secondary data must be supplemented by primary data originated specifically for the study at hand. Some common types of primary data are:

- demographic and socioeconomic characteristics
- psychological and lifestyle characteristics
- attitudes and opinions
- awareness and knowledge - for example, brand awareness
- intentions - for example, purchase intentions. While useful, intentions are not a reliable indication of actual future behaviour.
- motivation - a person's motives are more stable than his/her behaviour, so motive is a better predictor of future behaviour than is past behaviour.

Primary data can be obtained by communication or by

observation. Communication involves questioning respondents either verbally or in writing. This method is versatile, since one needs only to ask for the information; however, the response may not be accurate. Communication usually is quicker and cheaper than observation. Observation involves the recording of actions and is performed by either a person or some mechanical or electronic device. Observation is less versatile than communication since some attributes of a person may not be readily observable, such as attitudes, awareness, knowledge, intentions, and motivation. Observation also might take longer since observers may have to wait for appropriate events to occur, though observation using scanner data might be quicker and more cost effective. Observation typically is more accurate than communication.

Personal interviews have an interviewer bias that mail-in questionnaires do not have. For example, in a personal interview the respondent's perception of the interviewer may affect the responses.

Questionnaire Design

The questionnaire is an important tool for gathering primary data. Poorly constructed questions can result in large errors and invalidate the research data, so significant effort should be put into the questionnaire design. The questionnaire should be tested thoroughly prior to conducting the survey.

The questionnaire is a structured technique for collecting primary data in a marketing survey. It is a series of written or verbal questions for which the respondent provides answers. A well-designed questionnaire motivates the respondent to provide complete and accurate information. The survey questionnaire should not be viewed as a stand-alone tool. Along with the questionnaire there is field work, rewards for the respondents, and communication aids, all of which are important components of the questionnaire process.

Steps to Developing a Questionnaire

The following are steps to developing a questionnaire - the exact order may vary somewhat.

- Determine which information is being sought.
- Choose a question type (structure and amount of disguise) and method of administration (for example, written form, email or web form, telephone interview, verbal interview).
- Determine the general question content needed to obtain the desired information.
- Determine the form of response.
- Choose the exact question wording.
- Arrange the questions into an effective sequence.
- Specify the physical characteristics of the questionnaire (paper type, number of questions per page, etc.)
- Test the questionnaire and revise it as needed.

Required Information

To determine exactly which information is needed, it is useful to construct tables into which the data will be placed once it is collected. The tables will help to define what data is needed and what is not needed.

Question Type and Administration Method

Some question types include fixed alternative, open ended, and projective:

- Fixed-alternative questions provide multiple-choice answers. These types of questions are good when the possible replies are few and clear-cut, such as age, car ownership, etc.
- Open-ended questions allow the respondent to better express his/her answer, but are more difficult to administer and analyze. Often, open-ended questions are administered in a depth interview. This technique is most appropriate for exploratory research.
- Projective Methods use a vague question or stimulus and attempt to project a person's attitudes from the response. The questionnaire could use techniques such as word associations and fill-in-the-blank sentences. Projective methods are difficult to analyze and are better suited for exploratory research than for descriptive or causal research.

There are three commonly used rating scales: graphic, itemized, and comparative.

- Graphic - simply a line on which one marks an X anywhere between the extremes with an infinite number of places where the X can be placed.
- Itemized - similar to graphic except there are a limited number of categories that can be marked.

- Comparative - the respondent compares one attribute to others. Examples include the Q-sort technique and the constant sum method, which requires one to divide a fixed number of points among the alternatives. Questionnaires typically are administered via a personal or telephone interview or via a mail questionnaire.

Question Content

Each question should have a specific purpose or should not be included in the questionnaire. The goal of the questions is to obtain the required information. This is not to say that all questions directly must ask for the desired data. In some cases questions can be used to establish rapport with the respondent, especially when sensitive information is being sought.

Sensitive questions can be posed in ways to increase response likelihood and to facilitate more honest responses. Some techniques are:

- Place the question in a series of less personal questions.
- State that the behaviour or attitude is not so unusual.
- Phrase the question in terms of other people, not the respondent.
- Provide response choices that specify ranges, not exact numbers.
- Use a randomized response model giving the respondent pairs of questions with a randomly assigned one to answer. The interviewer does not know which question the person is answering, but

the overall percentage of people assigned to the sensitive question is known and statistics can be calculated.

Form of Question Response

Questions can be designed for open-ended, dichotomous, or multichotomous responses.

- Open-ended responses are difficult to evaluate, but are useful early in the research process for determining the possible range of responses.
- Dichotomous questions have two possible opposing responses, for example, "Yes" and "No".
- Multichotomous questions have a range of responses as in a multiple choice test.

The questionnaire designer should consider that respondents may not be able to answer some questions accurately. Two types of error are telescoping error and recall loss.

- *Telescoping error* is an error resulting from the tendency of people to remember events as occurring more recently than they actually did.
- *Recall loss* occurs when people forget that an event even occurred. For recent events, telescoping error dominates; for events that happened in the distant past, recall loss dominates.

Question Wording

The questions should be worded so that they are unambiguous and easily understood. The wording should consider the full context of the respondent's situation. In particular, consider the who, what, when, where, why, and how dimensions of the question.

For example, the question,

"Which brand of toothpaste do you use?"

might seem clear at first. However, the respondent may consider "you" to be the family as a whole rather than he or she personally. If the respondent recently changed brands, the "when" dimension of the question may be relevant. If the respondent uses a different, more compact tube of toothpaste when travelling, the "where" aspect of the question will matter.

A better wording of the question might be,

"Which brand of toothpaste have you used personally at home during the past 6 months? If you have used more than one brand, please list each of them."

When asking about the frequency of use, the questions should avoid ambiguous words such as "sometimes", "occasionally", or "regularly". Rather, more specific terms such as "once per day" and "2-3 times per week" should be used.

Sequence the Questions

Some neutral questions should be placed at the beginning of the questionnaire in order to establish rapport and put the respondent at ease. Effective opening questions are simple and non-threatening.

When sequencing the questions, keep in mind that their order can affect the response. One way to correct for this effect is to distribute half of the questionnaires with one order, and the other half with another order.

Physical Characteristics of the Questionnaire

Physical aspects such as the page layout, font type and size, question spacing, and type of paper should be considered. In order to eliminate the need to flip back and forth between pages, the layout should be designed so that a question at the bottom of the page does not need to be continued onto the next page. The font should be readable by respondents who have less-than-perfect visual acuity. The paper stock should be good quality to project the image that the questionnaire is important enough to warrant the respondents' time. Each questionnaire should have a unique number in order to better account for it and to know if any have been lost.

Test and Revise the Questionnaire

The questionnaire should be pre-tested in two stages before distributing. In the first stage, it should be administered using personal interviews in order to get better feedback on problems such as ambiguous questions. Then, it should be tested in the same way it will be administered. The data from the test should be analyzed the same way the administered data is to be analyzed in order to uncover any unanticipated shortcomings.

Different respondents will answer the same questionnaire differently. One hopes that the differences are due to real differences in the measured characteristics, but that often is not the case. Some sources of the differences between scores of different respondents are:

- True differences in the characteristic being measured.
- Differences in other characteristics such as response styles.
- Differences in transient personal factors such as fatigue, etc.
- Differences in situation, such as whether spouse is present.
- Differences in the administration, such as interviewer tone of voice.
- Differences resulting from sampling of items relevant toward the characteristic being measured.
- Differences resulting from lack of clarity of the question - may mean different things to different people.
- Differences caused by mechanical factors such as space to answer, inadvertent check marks, etc.

Measurement Scales

Attributes can be measured on nominal, ordinal, interval, and ratio scales:

- Nominal numbers are simply identifiers, with the only permissible mathematical use being for counting. Example: social security numbers.
- Ordinal scales are used for ranking. The interval between the numbers conveys no meaning. Median and mode calculations can be performed on ordinal numbers. Example: class ranking

- Interval scales maintain an equal interval between numbers. These scales can be used for ranking and for measuring the interval between two numbers. Since the zero point is arbitrary, ratios cannot be taken between numbers on an interval scale; however, mean, median, and mode are all valid. Example: temperature scale
- Ratio scales are referenced to an absolute zero values, so ratios between numbers on the scale are meaningful. In addition to mean, median, and mode, geometric averages also are valid. Example: weight

Validity and Reliability

The validity of a test is the extent to which differences in scores reflect differences in the measured characteristic. Predictive validity is a measure of the usefulness of a measuring instrument as a predictor. Proof of predictive validity is determined by the correlation between results and actual behaviour. Construct validity is the extent to which a measuring instrument measures what it intends to measure.

Reliability is the extent to which a measurement is repeatable with the same results. A measurement may be reliable and not valid. However, if a measurement is valid, then it also is reliable and if it is not reliable, then it cannot be valid. One way to show reliability is to show stability by repeating the test with the same results.

Attitude Measurement

Many of the questions in a marketing research survey are designed to measure attitudes. Attitudes are a person's general evaluation of something. Customer attitude is an important factor for the following reasons:

- Attitude helps to explain how ready one is to do something.
- Attitudes do not change much over time.
- Attitudes produce consistency in behaviour.
- Attitudes can be related to preferences.

Attitudes can be measured using the following procedures:

- Self-reporting - subjects are asked directly about their attitudes. Self-reporting is the most common technique used to measure attitude.
- Observation of behaviour - assuming that one's behaviour is a result of one's attitudes, attitudes can be inferred by observing behaviour. For example, one's attitude about an issue can be inferred by whether he/she signs a petition related to it.
- Indirect techniques - use unstructured stimuli such as word association tests.
- Performance of objective tasks - assumes that one's performance depends on attitude. For example, the subject can be asked to memorize the arguments of both sides of an issue. He/she is more likely to do a better job on the arguments that favour his/her stance.

- Physiological reactions - subject's response to a stimuli is measured using electronic or mechanical means. While the intensity can be measured, it is difficult to know if the attitude is positive or negative.
- Multiple measures - a mixture of techniques can be used to validate the findings, especially worthwhile when self-reporting is used.

There are several types of attitude rating scales:

- Equal-appearing interval scaling - a set of statements are assembled. These statements are selected according to their position on an interval scale of favourableness. Statements are chosen that has a small degree of dispersion. Respondents then are asked to indicate with which statements they agree.
- Likert method of summated ratings - a statement is made and the respondents indicate their degree of agreement or disagreement on a five point scale (Strongly Disagree, Disagree, Neither Agree Nor Disagree or undecided/indifferent, Agree, Strongly Agree).
- Semantic differential scale - a scale is constructed using phrases describing attributes of the product to anchor each end. For example, the left end may state, "Hours are inconvenient" and the right end may state, "Hours are convenient". The respondent then marks one of the seven blanks between the

statements to indicate his/her opinion about the attribute.
- Stapel Scale - similar to the semantic differential scale except that : 1) points on the scale are identified by numbers, 2) only one statement is used and if the respondent disagrees a negative number should marked, and 3) there are 10 positions instead of seven. This scale does not require that bipolar adjectives be developed and it can be administered by telephone.
- Q-sort technique - the respondent if forced to construct a normal distribution by placing a specified number of cards in one of 11 stacks according to how desirable he/she finds the characteristics written on the cards.

Sampling Plan

The sampling frame is the pool from which the interviewees are chosen. The telephone book often is used as a sampling frame, but have some shortcomings. Telephone books exclude those households that do not have telephones and those households with unlisted numbers. Since a certain percentage of the numbers listed in a phone book are out of service, there are many people who have just moved who are not sampled. Such sampling biases can be overcome by using random digit dialling. Mall intercepts represent another sampling frame, though there are many people who do not shop at malls and those who shop more often will be over-represented unless their answers are weighted in inverse proportion to their frequency of mall shopping.

In designing the research study, one should consider the potential errors. Two sources of errors *are random sampling error* and *non-sampling error*. Sampling errors are those due to the fact that there is a non-zero confidence interval of the results because of the sample size being less than the population being studied. Non-sampling errors are those caused by faulty coding, untruthful responses, respondent fatigue, etc.

There is a trade off between sample size and cost. The larger the sample size, the smaller the sampling error but the higher the cost. After a certain point the smaller sampling error cannot be justified by the additional cost.

While a larger sample size may reduce sampling error, it actually may increase the total error. There are two reasons for this effect. First, a larger sample size may reduce the ability to follow up on non-responses. Second, even if there is a sufficient number of interviewers for follow-ups, a larger number of interviewers may result in a less uniform interview process.

Data Collection

In addition to the intrinsic sampling error, the actual data collection process will introduce additional errors. These errors are called non-sampling errors. Some non-sampling errors may be intentional on the part of the interviewer, who may introduce a bias by leading the respondent to provide a certain response. The interviewer also may introduce unintentional errors, for example, due to not having a clear understanding of the interview process or due to fatigue.

Respondents also may introduce errors. A respondent may introduce intentional errors by lying or simply by not responding to a question. A respondent may introduce unintentional errors by not understanding the question, guessing, not paying close attention, and being fatigued or distracted.

Such non-sampling errors can be reduced through quality control techniques.

Data Analysis Preliminary Steps

Before analysis can be performed, raw data must be transformed into the right format. First, it must be edited so that errors can be corrected or omitted. The data must then be coded; this procedure converts the edited raw data into numbers or symbols. A codebook is created to document how the data was coded. Finally, the data is tabulated to count the number of samples falling into various categories. *Simple tabulations* count the occurrences of each variable independently of the other variables. *Cross tabulations*, also known as contingency tables or cross tabs, treats two or more variables simultaneously. However, since the variables are in a two-dimensional table, cross tabbing more than two variables is difficult to visualize since more than two dimensions would be required. Cross tabulation can be performed for nominal and ordinal variables.

Cross tabulation is the most commonly utilized data analysis method in marketing research. Many studies take the analysis no further than cross tabulation. This technique divides the sample into sub-groups to show how the dependent variable varies from one subgroup to another. A third variable can be introduced to uncover a relationship that initially was not evident.

Conjoint Analysis : The conjoint analysis is a powerful technique for determining consumer preferences for product attributes.

Hypothesis Testing : A basic fact about testing hypotheses is that a hypothesis may be rejected but that the hypothesis never can be unconditionally accepted until all possible evidence is evaluated. In the case of sampled data, the information set cannot be complete. So if a test using such data does not reject a hypothesis, the conclusion is not necessarily that the hypothesis should be accepted.

The null hypothesis in an experiment is the hypothesis that the independent variable has no effect on the dependent variable. The null hypothesis is expressed as H0. This hypothesis is assumed to be true unless proven otherwise. The alternative to the null hypothesis is the hypothesis that the independent variable does have an effect on the dependent variable. This hypothesis is known as the alternative, research, or experimental hypothesis and is expressed as H1. This alternative hypothesis states that the relationship observed between the variables cannot be explained by chance alone. There are two types of errors in evaluating hypotheses:

- Type I error: occurs when one rejects the null hypothesis and accepts the alternative, when in fact the null hypothesis is true.
- Type II error: occurs when one accepts the null hypothesis when in fact the null hypothesis is false.

Because their names are not very descriptive, these types

of errors sometimes are confused. Some people jokingly define a Type III error to occur when one confuses Type I and Type II. To illustrate the difference, it is useful to consider a trial by jury in which the null hypothesis is that the defendant is innocent. If the jury convicts a truly innocent defendant, a Type I error has occurred. If, on the other hand, the jury declares a truly guilty defendant to be innocent, a Type II error has occurred. Hypothesis testing involves the following steps:

- Formulate the null and alternative hypotheses.
- Choose the appropriate test.
- Choose a level of significance (alpha) - determine the rejection region.
- Gather the data and calculate the test statistic.
- Determine the probability of the observed value of the test statistic under the null hypothesis given the sampling distribution that applies to the chosen test.
- Compare the value of the test statistic to the rejection threshold.
- Based on the comparison, reject or do not reject the null hypothesis.
- Make the marketing research conclusion.

In order to analyze whether research results are statistically significant or simply by chance, a test of statistical significance can be run.

Tests of Statistical Significance

The chi-square (X^2) goodness-of-fit test is used to determine whether a set of proportions have specified numerical values. It often is used to analyze bivariate cross-tabulated data. Some examples of situations that are well-suited for this test are:

- A manufacturer of packaged products test markets a new product and wants to know if sales of the new product will be in the same relative proportion of package sizes as sales of existing products.
- A company's sales revenue comes from Product A (50%), Product B (30%), and Product C (20%). The firm wants to know whether recent fluctuations in these proportions are random or whether they represent a real shift in sales.

Chi-Square (X^2)

The chi-square test is performed by defining k categories and observing the number of cases falling into each category. Knowing the expected number of cases falling in each category, one can define chi-squared as:

$$X^2 = \sum (O_i - E_i)^2 / E_i$$

where

O_i = the number of observed cases in category i,
E_i = the number of expected cases in category i,
k = the number of categories,
the summation runs from $i = 1$ to $i = k$.

Before calculating the chi-square value, one needs to determine the expected frequency for each cell. This is done by dividing the number of samples by the number of cells in the table.

To use the output of the chi-square function, one uses a chi-square table. To do so, one needs to know the number of degrees of freedom (df). For chi-square applied to cross-tabulated data, the number of degrees of freedom is equal to (number of columns - 1) (number of rows - 1)

This is equal to the number of categories minus one. The conventional critical level of 0.05 normally is used. If the calculated output value from the function is greater than the chi-square look-up table value, the null hypothesis is rejected.

Spearman Rank Order Correlation (rho, r_s)

Another very popular statistical test among students is the Spearman rank order correlation. A research may like to investigate the presence or absence of association between variables of interest. For instance, he may like to know the association (relationship) between an employee's frequency of absenteeism and his age: he may want to know if age is directly or inversely related to the number of times the individual employee is absent in a year. If the older he is the more times he is absent, then we say that the association is direct, and if the older he is the less the number of times he is absent, we may conclude that there is an inverse relationship between age and absenteeism, etc.

We do not only want to know the type of relationship between the variables but also the strength of this relationship between them.

Assumptions

In using the Spearman rank order correlation (rho) we make the following necessary assumptions.

i. There are two variables of interest designated X (the assumed independent variable) and Y (the assumed dependent variable).

ii. There is a random sample of n pairs of X and Y observations either numeric or non numeric observations.

iii. Each x and each Y is ranked relative to all Xs and all Ys respectively and their ranks are denoted R(X) and R(Y), respectively.

iv. If ties occur, each tied value is assigned the mean of the rank for which it is tied, for example, if two values are both 21 and 21, and 21 occupies the 5th position in the ranking, then both values should occupy 5th and 6th positions since there are two 21. The mean of these two positions, 5th and 6th, is 5 + 6 divided by 2, that is, 5.5. Thus, each value should be assigned rank 5.5 in the array.

i. All the data or observations must be capable of being ranked.

Test Statistic of rho, r_s
The test statistics of Spearman rank order correlation, rs, is given as follows:

$$r_s = 1 - \frac{6 \sum d_i^2}{n(n^2.1)}$$

where

$$\sum_{i=1}^{n} d_i^2 = \sum_{i=1}^{n} R(X_1) - R(Y_1)^2$$

There are three possible relationships that can result from the computation of r_s.

These are"

    i. Perfect direct relationship, $r_s = +1$, when each pair of X and Y occupies the same rank in its respective X and Y ranking; $d_i^2 = 0$.

    ii. Perfect inverse relationships, $r_s = -1$, when the rank of one variable X and another variable Y within each pair of observations is the reverse of the other.

    iii. No relationship at all between the ranking of the pairs of x and Y within their respective observations, i. In this case the ranks of X_i have no relationship with the rank of Y_i.

Spearman rank order correlation hypotheses are either two-sided or one-sided. They take the following format:

i. Two sided hypothesis

    Ho: X and Y are not related

    H_1:   X and Y are directly or indirectly related

ii. One sided hypothesis

    Ho: X and Y are not related

    H_1:   X and y are directly related

iii. One-sided hypothesis
   Ho: X and Y are not related

   H_1:   X and Y are inversely related.

Decision Rule

For two – sided hypothesis, reject H_o at the appropriate ∝ level, if the computed rs is greater than the critical ∝ value corresponding to 1 - ∝/2.

Even by inspection one can conclude whether the correlation is positive, negative, high or low. Certainly, a 0.70 correlation can be said to be positive, and high but not perfect just as a 0.30 correlation can be said to be positive and low. All the same, we may use the critical values of Spearman test statistic in a standard statistics text to test the correlation between X and Y variables.

If, however, we want to know the strength of the relationship between X and Y variables, we may convert the Spearman rank correlation statistics to t statistics using the following formula:

$$t = r_s \sqrt{\frac{n-2}{1-r_s^2}}$$

Then use the result to test the hypothesis. The t statistic can be used only when the number of sample-pairs is equal to or greater than 10. Otherwise only Spearman rank order correlation is used.

Example

In a recent study carried out by a student (for his degree project) on operational problems of a Lagos based multi-national organisation, the intention was to know if the company's expenditure on sales promotion was associated with its sales. He obtained the following data.

Table 3.2: Sales and Sales Costs of Company B 1976 – 85.

Year	Sales (₦m)	Sales Promotion Cost (₦m)
1976	8.06	0.06
1977	10.61	0.08
1978	11.14	0.13
1979	13.72	0.16
1980	16.22	0.18
1981	18.89	0.21
1982	16.51	0.18
1983	11.50	0.08
1984	10.21	0.09
1985	14.27	0.16

(Source: Student's B.Sc.) Project, Unilag 1986).

The research problem here is to find if there is a relationship between sales revenue and sales promotion costs. The following hypotheses were tested:

H_o: There is no direct relationship between sales revenue of company B for the period, 19765 – 1985, and sales promotion costs for the same period

H_1: There is a direct relationship between sales revenue of company B for the period, 19765 – 1985, and sales promotion costs for the same period.

The tests were carried out at $\alpha = 0.05$.

The test statistic, $r_s = \dfrac{6 \sum d^2}{N(n^2-1)}$ was computed as follows:

Table 3.3: Relationship Between Sales Revenue and Sales Promotion Costs for the Same Period (19765 – 1985).

	(₦m) Y	(₦m) X	R(Yi)	R(xi)	(R(x) – R(y)) Di	O
1976	0.06	0.06	1	1	0	0
1977	10.61	0.08	3	2.5	-0.5	0.25
1978	11.14	0.13	4	5	1.0	1.0
1979	13.72	0.16	6	6.5	0.5	0.25
1980	16.22	0.18	8	8.5	0.5	0.25
1981	18.89	0.21	10	10	.0	.0
1982	16.51	0.18	9	8.5	-0.5	0.25
1983	11.50	0.08	5	2.5	-2.5	6.25
1984	10.21	0.09	2	4	2.0	4.00
1985	14.27	0.16	7	6.5	-0.5	0.25
					$Di^2 =$	12.2

$$\begin{aligned}
Rs &= 1 - \dfrac{6 \sum d^2}{n(n^2 - 1)} \\
&= 1 - \dfrac{(6)(12.5)}{10(100-1)} \\
&= 1 - \dfrac{75}{99} \\
&= 1 - 0.076 \\
&= \underline{0.924}
\end{aligned}$$

This shows almost a perfect correlation between sales revenue and cost of sales promotion. Let us now examine the strength of this positive correlation by converting the r_s value to t scores, thus:

$$t = r_s \sqrt{\frac{n-2}{1-r_s^2}}$$

$$= 0.924 \sqrt{\frac{10-2}{1-(0.924)^2}}$$

$$= 0.924 \sqrt{\frac{8}{1-0.854}}$$

$$= 0.924 \sqrt{\frac{8}{0.146}}$$

$$= 0.924 \sqrt{54.79}$$

$$= (0.924)(7.40)$$

$$= \underline{6.84}$$

Degrees of Freedom = n-2 = 10-2 = 8

The critical value of t for $\alpha = 0.05$ and 8 degrees of freedom is 2.306.

Thus, t = 6.84 t_{995} = 2.306 at 8 df. Decision: Reject H_o at α 0.05 and accept H_1; that is, there is a direct positive relationship between company B's sales revenue and its cost of sales promotion.

ANOVA

Another test of significance is the Analysis of Variance (ANOVA) test. The primary purpose of ANOVA is to test for differences between multiple means. Whereas the t-test can be used to compare two means, ANOVA is needed to compare three or more means. If multiple t-tests were applied, the probability of a TYPE I error (rejecting a true null hypothesis) increases as the number of comparisons increases.

One-way ANOVA examines whether multiple means differ. The test is called an F-test. ANOVA calculates the ratio of the variation between groups to the variation within groups (the F ratio). While ANOVA was designed for comparing several means, it also can be used to compare two means. Two-way ANOVA allows for a second independent variable and addresses interaction.

To run a one-way ANOVA, use the following steps:

1. Identify the independent and dependent variables.
2. Describe the variation by breaking it into three parts - the total variation, the portion that is within groups, and the portion that is between groups (or among groups for more than two groups). The total variation (SS_{total}) is the sum of the squares of the differences between each value and the grand mean of all the values in all the groups. The in-group variation (SS_{within}) is the sum of the squares of the differences in each element's value and the group mean. The variation between group means ($SS_{between}$) is the total variation minus the in-group variation ($SS_{total} - SS_{within}$).

3. Measure the difference between each group's mean and the grand mean.
4. Perform a significance test on the differences.
5. Interpret the results.

This F-test assumes that the group variances are approximately equal and that the observations are independent. It also assumes normally distributed data; however, since this is a test on means the Central Limit Theorem holds as long as the sample size is not too small.

ANOVA is efficient for analyzing data using relatively few observations and can be used with categorical variables. Note that regression can perform a similar analysis to that of ANOVA.

Discriminant Analysis Analysis of the difference in means between groups provides information about individual variables, it is not useful for determining their individual impacts when the variables are used in combination. Since some variables will not be independent from one another, one needs a test that can consider them simultaneously in order to take into account their interrelationship. One such test is to construct a linear combination, essentially a weighted sum of the variables. To determine which variables discriminate between two or more naturally occurring groups, discriminant analysis is used. Discriminant analysis can determine which variables are the best predictors of group membership. It determines which groups differ with respect to the mean of a variable, and then uses that variable to predict new cases of group membership. Essentially, the discriminant function problem is a one-way ANOVA problem in that one can determine whether multiple groups are significantly different from one another with respect to the mean of a particular variable.

A discriminant analysis consists of the following steps:

1. Formulate the problem.
2. Determine the discriminant function coefficients that result in the highest ratio of between-group variation to within-group variation.
3. Test the significance of the discriminant function.
4. Interpret the results.
5. Determine the validity of the analysis.

Discriminant analysis analyzes the dependency relationship, whereas factor analysis and cluster analysis address the interdependency among variables.

Factor Analysis

Factor analysis is a very popular technique to analyze interdependence. Factor analysis studies the entire set of interrelationships without defining variables to be dependent or independent.

Factor analysis combines variables to create a smaller set of factors. Mathematically, a factor is a linear combination of variables. A factor is not directly observable; it is inferred from the variables. The technique identifies underlying structure among the variables, reducing the number of variables to a more manageable set. Factor analysis groups variables according to their correlation.

The *factor loading* can be defined as the correlations between the factors and their underlying variables. A factor loading matrix is a key output of the factor analysis. An example matrix is shown below:

Table 3.4: Factor Analysis

Variable	Factor 1	Factor 2	Factor 3
Variable 1			
Variable 2			
Variable 3			
Column's Sum of Squares:			

Each cell in the matrix represents correlation between the variable and the factor associated with that cell. The square of this correlation represents the proportion of the variation in the variable explained by the factor. The sum of the squares of the factor loadings in each column is called an eigenvalue. An eigenvalue represents the amount of variance in the original variables that is associated with that factor. The *communality* is the amount of the variable variance explained by common factors.

A rule of thumb for deciding on the number of factors is that each included factor must explain at least as much variance as does an average variable. In other words, only factors for which the eigenvalue is greater than one are used. Other criteria for determining the number of factors include the Screen plot criteria and the percentage of variance criteria.

To facilitate interpretation, the axis can be rotated. Rotation of the axis is equivalent to forming linear combinations of the factors. A commonly used rotation strategy is the *varimax* rotation. Varimax attempts to force the column entries to be either close to zero or one.

Cluster Analysis

Market segmentation usually is based not on one factor but on multiple factors. Initially, each variable represents its own cluster. The challenge is to find a way to combine variables so that relatively homogenous clusters can be formed. Such clusters should be internally homogenous and externally heterogeneous. Cluster analysis is one way to accomplish this goal. Rather than being a statistical test, it is more of a collection of algorithms for grouping objects, or in the case of marketing research, grouping people. Cluster analysis is useful in the exploratory phase of research when there are no a-priori hypotheses.

Cluster analysis steps:

1. Formulate the problem, collecting data and choosing the variables to analyze.

2. Choose a distance measure. The most common is the Euclidean distance. Other possibilities include the squared Euclidean distance, city-block (Manhattan) distance, Chebychev distance, power distance, and percent disagreement.
3. Choose a clustering procedure (linkage, nodal, or factor procedures).
4. Determine the number of clusters. They should be well separated and ideally they should be distinct enough to give them descriptive names such as professionals, buffs, etc.
5. Profile the clusters.
6. Assess the validity of the clustering.

Marketing Research Report

The format of the marketing research report varies with the needs of the organization. The report often contains the following sections:

- Authorization letter for the research
- Table of Contents
- List of illustrations
- Executive summary
- Research objectives
- Methodology
- Results
- Limitations
- Conclusions and recommendations
- Appendices containing copies of the questionnaire, etc.

Marketing research by itself does not arrive at marketing

decisions, nor does it guarantee that the organization will be successful in marketing its products. However, when conducted in a systematic, analytical, and objective manner, marketing research can reduce the uncertainty in the decision-making process and increase the probability and magnitude of success.

CHAPTER 4

SCOPE OF STRATEGIC MARKETING

Marketing is a philosophy that leads to the process by which organizations, groups and individuals obtain what they need and want by identifying value, providing it, communicating it and delivering it to others. The core concepts of marketing are customers' needs, wants and values; products, exchange, communications and relationships. Marketing is strategically concerned with the direction and scope of the long-term activities performed by the organization to obtain a competitive advantage. The organization applies its resources within a changing environment to satisfy customer needs while meeting stakeholder expectations. Implied in this view of strategic marketing is the requirement to develop a strategy to cope with competitors, identify market opportunities, develop and commercialize new products and services, allocate resources among marketing activities and design an appropriate organizational structure to ensure the performance desired is achieved. There is no unique strategy that succeeds for all organizations in all situations. In thinking strategically about marketing many factors must be considered: the extent of product diversity and geographic coverage in the organization; the number of market segments served, marketing channels used, the role of branding, the level of marketing effort, and the role of quality. It is also necessary to consider the organization's approach to new product development, in particular, its position as a technology leader or follower, the extent of innovation, the organization's cost position and pricing policy, and its relationship to customers, competitors, suppliers and partners. The challenge of strategic marketing is, therefore, to manage marketing complexity, customer and stakeholder expectations and to reconcile the influences of a changing environment in the context of a set of resource capabilities. It is also necessary to create strategic opportunities and to manage the concomitant changes required within the organization. In this world of marketing, organizations seek to maximize returns to shareholders by creating a competitive advantage in identifying, providing, communicating and delivering value to customers, broadly defined, and in the process developing long-term mutually satisfying relationships with those customers.

Understanding Marketing – Antecedents

The fundamental management issue in marketing is to determine a superior value position from the customer's perspective and to ensure that, by developing a consensus throughout the organization, value is provided, communicated and delivered to the customer group. The core concepts of marketing are needs, wants and demands which directly affect the identification and selection of relevant customer values reflected in products, services and ideas that the organization provides, communicates and delivers in the form of exchanges to build long-term satisfactory relationships with customers (Figure 4.1). Needs are the internal influences which prompt behaviour, e.g. biological needs refer to a person's requirements for food, air and shelter while social needs refer to issues such as security, personal gratification and prestige. Wants are culture bound and may be satisfied using a number of technologies, e.g. a teenager may listen to music on one of the rock radio stations or on

DVDs played on a computer. Demand refers to the ability and willingness of a customer to buy a particular product or service which satisfies the want and the more latent need. A student may want a BMW but can afford only a bicycle. The organization may set out from the start or be established with those objectives or, more likely, as a result of trial and error and experience, the organization evolves into a position over time of being the desired source of value. The core concepts of marketing may be decomposed into a number of basic components:

Figure 4.1: Core concepts of marketing

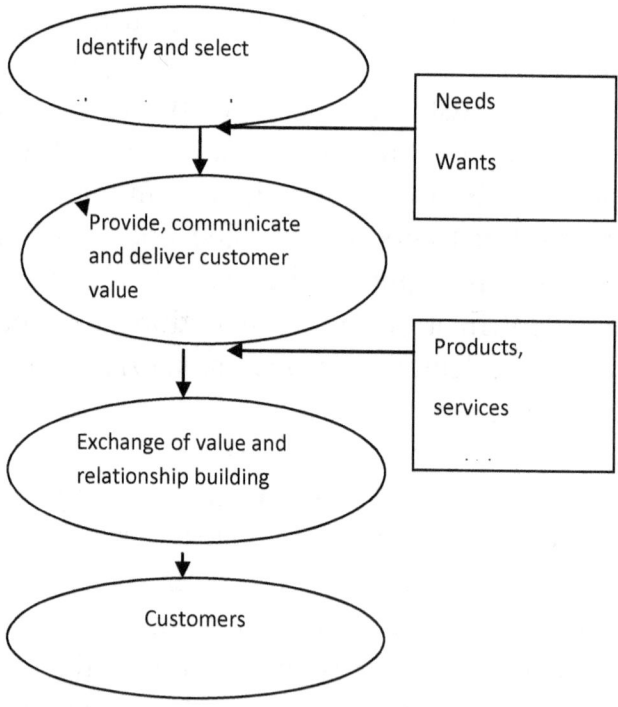

- Provide the value

– product planning

– packaging

– branding

– pricing

_ Communicate the value

– advertising

– personal selling

– direct marketing

– sales promotion

_ Deliver the value

– channels of distribution

– logistics

– servicing.

Successful organizations recognize value positions and ensure that learning occurs throughout the organization as a result of discovering the value position. Choosing the value position is one of the most important strategic decisions facing the organization. Once chosen, it the task of management to ensure that everyone in the organization directly contributes to delivering the chosen value.

Marketing and sales orientations: A sales emphasis is very different from a marketing emphasis in the organization. Four important areas where they differ separate the two approaches: organizational objectives, orientation, attitudes to segmentation and the perceived task facing marketing in the organization (Kotler 2002). A sales emphasis results in objectives which are aimed at increasing current sales to meet quotas and to derive commissions and bonuses. Little discrimination is made between products or customers in terms of profits unless these differences are written into the incentives. In contrast, objectives with a marketing emphasis take profits into account. Marketing objectives include an explicit consideration of product mixes, customer groups and different communications and ways of reaching the market in attempting to achieve profitable sales and market shares at acceptable levels of risk. The selling and marketing orientations produce very different emphases in the organization. A selling orientation predominantly reflects a production approach whereby something is produced and the task is to sell it thereby.

Figure 4.2: Alternative Business Orientation of the Firm

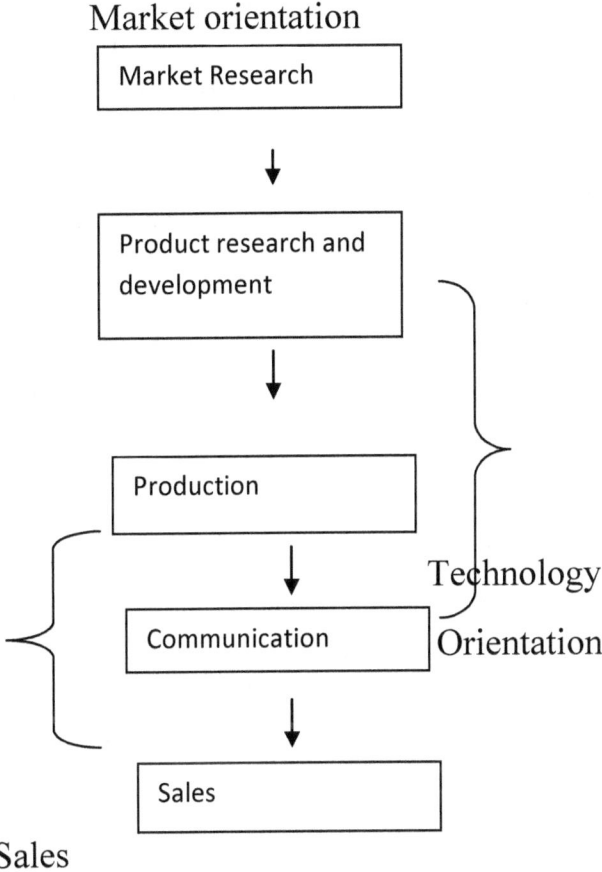

A focus on sales means a focus on individual customers rather than market segments or market classes. Such organizations are very knowledgeable about individual accounts and the variables which influence specific sales transactions but they are less interested in developing an approach to an entire segment of similar needs and wants in the market.

A technology orientation is similar to a sales orientation except that the organization also engages in product research and development (Figure 4.2). A marketing approach attempts to determine ways of offering superior value to the more profitable segments without damaging individual customer relationships. A marketing approach reflects an integrated approach based on research and feedback. Customer needs are first evaluated through market research, an integrated marketing effort is developed to satisfy customers so that the organization achieves its goals, especially those affecting shareholders. This is a customer orientation and contrasts very bluntly with a narrow competitor orientation based on sales in which the organization by capitalizing on the weaknesses of vulnerable competitors or by removing its own competitive weaknesses attempts to obtain high sales and long-run profits (Figure 4.3). In many situations marketing evaluates itself and presents its case to senior managers of the organization based on sales, efficiency or, worst of all, internal awards, not marketplace outcomes or financial success. Senior managers deal with issues that involve the allocation of resources and how such allocation affects the return on investment. These hurdle rates are calculated differently from one organization to another but they need to be understood for a marketing programmeme to be effective and accepted. In a business world dominated by financial considerations the ability of the organization to produce award-winning marketing programmemes or attractive but fuzzy images in TV commercials is not of much value. Traditional marketing thinking assumes that the organization is in complete control of the marketplace, whereas interaction and market integration are required.

Figure 4.3: Customer and competitor orientation in the organization

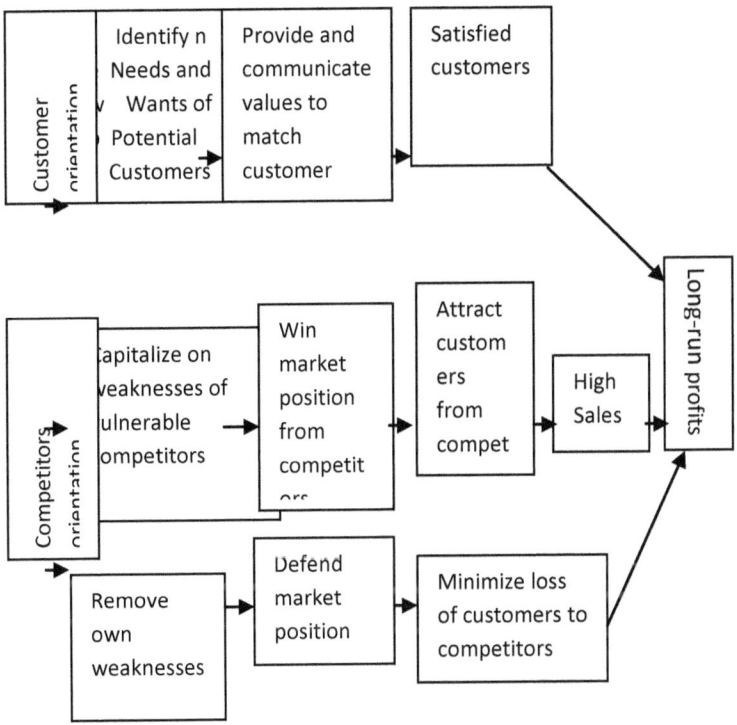

Source: Adapted from Alfred R. Oxfenfeldt and William L. Moore

Strategic Marketing Concept Marketing has been defined as the management function responsible for identifying, anticipating and satisfying customer requirements profitably. Marketing is, therefore, both a philosophy and a set of techniques which address such matters as research, product design and development, pricing, packaging, sales and sales promotion, advertising, public relations, distribution and after-sales service. These activities define the broad scope of marketing and their balanced integration within a marketing plan is known as the marketing mix. A modification of a definition of marketing by Doyle (2000) suggests that marketing is the management process that seeks to maximize returns to shareholders by creating a competitive advantage in providing, communicating and delivering value to customers thereby developing a long-term relationship with them. This definition clearly defines the objectives of marketing and how its performance should be evaluated. The specific contribution of marketing in the organization lies in the formulation of strategies to choose the right customer, build relationships of trust with them and create a competitive advantage (Doyle 2000, p. 235). A marketing strategy consists of an internally integrated but externally focused set of choices about how the organization addresses its customers in the context of a competitive environment. A strategy has five elements: it deals with where the organization plans to be active; how it will get there; how it will succeed in the marketplace; what the speed and sequence of moves will be; and how the organization will obtain profits

(Hambrick and Fredrickson 2001, p. 50).

The organization must identify the problem that its customers use its products and services to solve. It is also necessary to identify the benefits customers seek from using a product or service available in the market. A market consists of all the potential customers who share a particular need or want who might be willing and able to engage in exchange to satisfy that need or want. A marketing orientation helps to define the organization's business. Marketing is concerned with problem solving and customer benefits. The organization must be able to answer the following questions:

_ What is the problem customers are trying to solve?

_ What benefits do customers seek?

_ How well does the organization's product solve this problem and provide these benefits?

A statement that the organization is in the movie business is not very useful. An organization is not in the movie business because that says nothing about customer needs. Some movie organizations assumed they were in the movie business when the entertainment business left them behind! Marketing is a philosophy that encourages the organization to ensure that the needs and wants of customers in selected target markets are reflected in all its actions and activities while recognizing constraints imposed by society. This marketing concept first received formal recognition in 1952 by one of its leading exponents, the General Electric Organization – the marketing concept:

... introduces the marketing man at the beginning rather than at the end of the production cycle and integrates marketing into each phase of business. . . . marketing establishes . . . for the engineer, the design and manufacturing man, what the customer wants in a given product, what price he is willing to pay and where and when it will be wanted. Marketing will have authority in product planning, production scheduling and inventory control, as well as in sales distribution or servicing of the product (General Electric Organization, New York, 1952, Annual Report, p. 21). Three aspects of this statement are interesting: the customer orientation; the profit orientation; and the emphasis on integrated organization effort. These three aspects are fundamental to the adoption of the marketing concept. Marketing means, therefore, being oriented to the needs of customers rather than emphasizing what is convenient to produce. Effective marketing requires that the organization analyses the needs that its products are supposed to satisfy. Customers do not buy 'coffee'; they buy a warm stimulating drink or a unique café experience if it is Starbucks. Likewise, customers do not buy sisal; they buy a material to make baling rope to tie things together or fibre to serve as backing for a floor covering. The organization should realize that many alternative products may satisfy the needs identified; there usually are many substitutes – for coffee include tea, cocoa, alcohol or soft drinks and for sisal include polypropylene fibre or polythene sheeting. The real lesson of a marketing philosophy is that better performing organizations recognize the basic and enduring nature of the customer needs they are attempting to satisfy. It is the technology of want satisfaction which is transitory

(Anderson 1982, p. 23). The products and services used to satisfy customer needs and wants change constantly. The adoption of a marketing philosophy confers specific authority and responsibility within the organization in regard to the provision, communication and delivery of customer value. Marketing is concerned with all parts of the organization; it is more than a set of tools, it is an orientation which pervades the thinking of the organization as a whole. Internal marketing In addition to equipping the organization to cope with the outside world of customers and competitors, it is also necessary to train and motivate all staff within the organization to provide the appropriate level of service to customers. Internal marketing is very closely related to human resource management and the way in which the organization develops its own distinctive corporate culture. Internal marketing is the task of successfully hiring, training and motivating able employees who want to serve customers well. It is obvious that it is necessary to determine the organization's internal culture before venturing forth to serve customers in the external world. This internal market must be motivated to react in a certain desired way which is best described as marketing-like (Gronroos 1984, p. 3).

Internal marketing helps employees make a strong connection to the products and services sold by the organization. Without such a connection employees may unwittingly undermine expectations set by the organization's marketing communications. When people believe in what the organization does and stands for, they are motivated to work harder and their loyalty to the organization increases. According to Mitchell (2002), however, in most organizations internal marketing is done poorly, if at all, and few organizations understand the need to convince employees of the organization's mission and purpose; they take it for granted. Since satisfying customers is central to the task of marketing, it is essential that everybody in the organization who deals with customers must be imbued with a sense of marketing which means internal marketing for some and external marketing for others. Customers exist, therefore, both within and outside the organization. By focusing on customers, in this way a different perspective of the organization is obtained. In traditional organizations the chief executive and senior manager appear at the top of the chart with sales and other front-office people at the bottom. In many such charts customers are not represented at all. A contrary view, driven by a strong sense of marketing and especially internal marketing places the customer on top, the front-office people next, middle managers below that and finally senior managers (Figure 4.4). As the front-office people meet and serve customers, they should receive a lot of attention within the organization.

Figure 4.4: Internal marketing and customer orientation

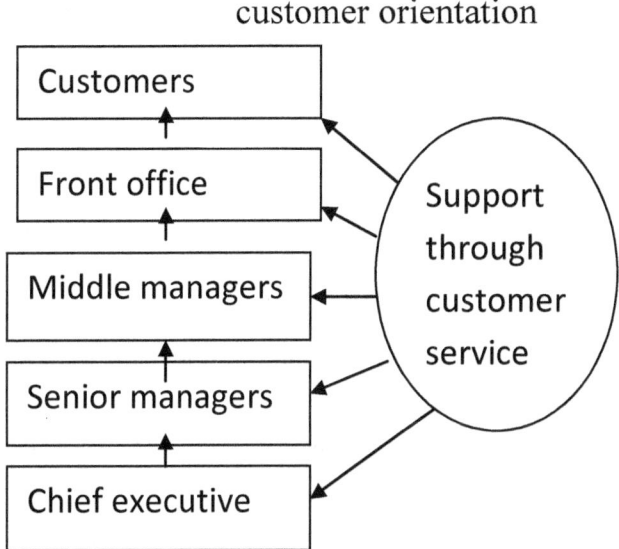

Middle managers exist, in this view of the world, to support the layer of middle level operators. It is important to note that everybody is somebody else's customer. That is why the customer is placed on top and is so important to the survival and growth of the organization.

Strategic Marketing in Action In its strategic role, marketing focuses on a business's intentions in a market and the means and timing of realizing those intentions. The strategic role of marketing is quite different from marketing management, which deals with developing, implementing, and directing programmes to achieve designated intentions. To clearly differentiate between marketing management and marketing in its new role, a new term – strategic marketing – has been coined to represent the latter. This section discusses different aspects of strategic marketing and examines how it differs from marketing management. Also noted are the trends pointing to the continued importance of strategic marketing.

Marketing function plays strategic role at different levels in the organization. At the corporate level, marketing inputs (e.g., competitive analysis, market dynamics, and environmental shifts) are essential for formulating a corporate strategic plan. Marketing represents the boundary between the market-place and the company and knowledge of current and emerging happenings in the marketplace is extremely important in any strategic planning exercise. At the other end of the scale, marketing management deals with the formulation and implementation of marketing programmes to support the perspectives of strategic marketing, referring to marketing strategy of a product/market. Marketing strategy is developed at the business unit level.

Within a given environment, marketing strategy deals essentially with the interplay of three forces known as the strategic three Cs: the customer, the competition, and the corporation. Marketing strategies focus on ways in which the corporation can differentiate itself effectively from its competitors, capitalizing on its distinctive strengths to deliver better value to its customers. A good marketing strategy should be characterized by:

(a) a clear market definition
(b) a good match between corporate strengths and the needs of the market and

(c) superior performance, relative to the competition, in the key success factors of the business.

Figure 4.5: Strategic Marketing Concept

Thus, marketing strategy is the creation of a unique and valuable position, involving a different set of activities. Thus, development of marketing strategy requires choosing activities that are different from rivals.

The concept of strategic marketing may be illustrated with reference to the introduction by Gillette Company of a new shaving product; Mach 3 in April 1998. For some time, *Gillette* had faced slow growth in its razor's division, partly because *Schick*, its smaller rival, had recently launched a new razor of its own. Investors had begun to fret about slowing growth and lackluster sales at Gillette. This threatened its basic business, that is razor and blades market, in which it had 71% of the North Nigerian and European market. Apparently, *Gillette* needed a new marketing strategy to protect its razor and blades territory. Looking around, Gillette decided to introduce a new razor that its research laboratory had been developing and that was ready to be launched. *Gillette* had an unusual approach to innovation. Most companies tweaked their offerings in response to competition or demand. *Gillette* launched a new product only when it had made a genuine technical advance. To make the Mach 3, Gillette had found a way to bond diamond-hard carbon to silvers of steel. The time was on *Gillette*'s side. It needed something revolutionary to strengthen its market position and its research laboratory had a unique product ready to be launched Gillette delineated the following marketing strategy:

- Market (where to compete) – *Gillette* decided to introduce Mach 3 throughout the U. S. on the same day.
- Means (how to compete) – *Gillette* decided to offer Mach 3 as a premium product that was priced 35% more than Sensor Excel, which itself was 60% more expensive that Atra, its predecessor. Gillette reasoned "People never remember what they used to pay. But they want to feel they are getting value for money."
- Timing (when to compete) – Gillette decided to introduce the new product before its CEO, Mr Al

Zien, retired. Mr Zien's ability to communicate had been a hit on both Wall Street and in the company. Much of the Gillette's recent success was attributed to Mr Zien and the company wanted Mach 3 to adequately settle in a dominant position before Mr Zein retired.

Gillette's Mach 3 strategy emerged from a thorough consideration of the strategic three Cs. First, market entry was dictated by customers' willingness to adopt new products in the toiletry field. Eight years ago, Gillette was losing its grip on the razor market to cheap throwaways. Sensor, which replaced Atra razor, saved the company. The company was hopeful that the Mach 3 would have a similar effect. Second, the decision to enter the market was based on full knowledge of the competition, which included its own substitute products, such as Sensor and Atra shavers, as well as companies like Schick. The company was more concerned about its own products competing with Mach 3, and therefore it ran down stocks of its Sensor and Atra shavers ahead of Mach 3's launch. Third, Gillette's strength as an aggressive successful marketer of packaged goods with is vast experience in shaving products business and adequate financial resources (Gillette spent over $750 million in developing Mach 3) properly equipped it to enter the market. Finally, the environment (in this case a trend toward acceptance of technologically advanced products; Mach 3 was covered by 35 patents) substantiated the opportunity.

This strategy seems to have worked well for *Gillette*.

In nine months ending 1998, Gillette shaving products sales were up 28%. And yet, the company has to introduce the product in Europe (with 71% market) as well as in developing countries (Latin America, where the company has 91% market for blades and India with 69% of the market). Inasmuch as Gillette did not tailor its product to local peculiarities, it was able to achieve vast economies of scale in manufacturing. The economies of scale were mirrored on the distribution side as well. The company usually broke into new markets with razors and then jumped into batteries, pens, and toiletries through the established sales channels.

Importance of Strategic Marketing

Strategic thinking represents a new perspective in the area of marketing. In this section we will examine the importance, characteristics, origin and future of strategic marketing. Marketing plays a vital role in the strategic management process of a firm. The experience of companies well versed in strategic planning indicates that failure in marketing can block the way to goals established by the strategic plan. A prime example is provided by Texas Instruments, a pioneer in developing a system of strategic planning called the OST system. Marketing negligence forced Texas instruments to withdraw from the digital watch business. When the external environment is stable, a company can successfully ride on its technological lead, manufacturing efficiency, and financial acumen. As the environment shifts, however, lack of marketing perspective makes the best-planned strategies treacherous. With the intensification of competition in the watch business and the loss of uniqueness of the digital watch. Texas Instruments began to lose ground. Its experience can be summarized as follows:

The lack of marketing skills certainly was a major factor in the ... demise of its watch business. T. I. did not try to understand the consumer, nor would it listen to the marketplace. They had the engineer's attitude. Philip Morris's success with Miller Beer illustrates how marketing's elevated strategic status can help in outperforming competitors. If Philip Morris had accepted the conventional marketing wisdom of the beer industry by basing its strategy on cost efficiencies of large breweries and competitive pricing, its Miller Beer subsidiary might still be in seventh place or lower. Instead, Miller Beer leapfrogged all competitors but Anheuser-Busch by emphasizing market and customer segmentation supported with large advertising and promotion budgets. A case of true strategic marketing, with the marketing function playing a crucial role in overall corporate strategy, Philip Morris relied on its corporate strengths and exploited its competitors' weaknesses to gain a leadership position in the brewing industry.

Indeed, marketing strategy is the most significant challenge that companies of all types and sizes face. As a study by Enyioko and Etim, (2006) notes, "Nigerian corporations are beginning to answer a new call to strategic marketing, 'as many of them shift their business planning priorities more toward strategic marketing and the market planning function.

Responsibility in Marketing

Marketing should distinguish between the individual customer's short-term needs and wants and the longer-term welfare of society. For example, large cars greatly contribute to the pollution and traffic congestion of cities and cigarettes cause major health problems, even death, for smokers and for those who inhale the smoke. It is necessary, therefore, to integrate profitability requirements with health, ecological and environmental constraints. For many years writers on marketing have been at pains to point out that the principal function of marketing 'is not so much to be skilful in making the customer do what suits the interests of the business as to be skilled in conceiving and then making the business do what suits the interests of the customers' (McKittrick 1957, p. 78). In a present-day context, to be skilful in conceiving the real interests of customers, the organization must balance environmental considerations against profitability requirements; society's welfare against individual needs; and the long-term welfare of customers against their short-term wants. For these reasons, therefore, we must broaden the marketing concept to include wider dimensions. The two major assumptions behind marketing are that consumers know what they want and are informed and highly rational in satisfying their wants, and that customer sovereignty prevails (Dickinson et al. 1986, p. 9). These authors argue that if the organization were right in assuming that customers know what they want, then the key issue would be to create the product, create awareness of it and make it available at an acceptable price. The fact is that both goals and corresponding wants can be unstable, with wants being only vaguely articulated as consumers remain open to persuasion as to what might better serve their interests (Dickinson *et al.* 1986, p. 20). This is especially true in high technology markets where new product development is frequently technology driven. The marketing concept also assumes that the customer is sovereign, i.e. organizations follow the dictates of the market in regard to exactly what should be provided. But customers do not always know exactly what they want and they may be unsure of their trade-offs among product or service attributes. Many organizations see no inconsistency in referring to marketing as the basis for management while at the same time accepting that customer perceptions are important and can be influenced.

Social and Ethical Constraints Social responsibility in marketing means accounting for the relationship between marketing and the environment in which it operates. Social responsibility refers to the obligation of the organization, beyond the requirements of the law, to take into practical consideration in its decision making the social consequences of its decisions and actions, as well as profits. This view of social responsibility implies constraints on the organization more rigorous than arise if the organization attempted to fulfill its economic and legal requirements only. The reasons for a greater interest in social responsibility stem from the greater involvement of business with government and the influence of myriad stakeholders in the organization: shareholders, institutional investors, employees and other regulatory and environmental bodies. The more important dimensions of the environment which relate to an appropriate application of marketing are the social and moral environment, the business environment and the physical environment. In recent years ethical issues, social and moral standards which are acceptable in a society, have become very important in marketing. Trust is a related issue which is an essential ingredient in building long-term relationships between organizations and their customers. Trust is well placed where ethical standards are upheld. It is misplaced where ethical standards are ignored or flaunted. Both trust and ethics are highly dependent on culture and vary according to the culture and background of customers. Organizations operating in many cultures have greater difficulty in coping with a heterogeneous set of customers, drawing on disparate cultures for their ethical standards. One example will illustrate the issue. In a questionable practice, with strong implications for marketing responsibility, advertising agencies in the US have begun to assist pharmaceutical organizations to recruit patients for clinical trials. According to Thomas Harrison, the Omnicom Group, Inc., parent organization of advertising agency BBDO Worldwide, BBD Worldwide and TBWA Worldwide:

What you're seeing is an emergency convergence between clinical development and the commercialization of drugs. The ultimate goal is to make drug development more efficient. What we want to try to do is look at the molecule in the test tube as a brand. A lot of people don't think a brand is a brand until it has FDA (Food and Drug Administration) approval. But we are asking, 'What is the maximum commercial potential of this molecule? What will it be when it grows up? What is the message? How should the clinical trial be developed?' (The Wall

Street Journal Europe, Friday, Saturday, Sunday 15–17 March 2002, p. A 10). There is potentially a real ethical clash of science and business in such a development.

There are clear benefits for the advertising agency as becoming involved early in the process can be lucrative and can greatly increase the chance of acquiring the account if the product is ultimately launched. For the pharmaceutical organization the involvement of the agency can shorten the time and costly process of getting a drug from development to market. In these circumstances there could be a temptation for the agency to modify the test results or at least present them in such a way as to favour the pharmaceutical organization in anticipation of eventually being retained to produce the advertising campaign and thus obtain high advertising fees. This is a conflict of interest – a potentially controversial practice that directly raises ethical questions for marketing. Environmental responsibility in marketing The view that marketing has a special responsibility when discussing the natural environment is also well developed. By promoting product manufacture and usage, the organization may be encouraging resource depletion, pollution or other environmental deterioration. Most organizations believe that it is not sufficient to make profits and generate employment while ignoring an obligation to society regarding the preservation of the natural environment even though their behaviour is within the law. Some organizations, however, continue to ignore this implied obligation claiming that their behaviour is not illegal when they dump chemicals in watercourses, over-package products, or damage the atmosphere. Such organizations often cite a concern for the feasibility rather than the propriety of believing that they should not be expected to take action to protect the environment if their competitive position were to be jeopardized. In a general way, social responsibility is an investment in future profits which should be made even at the expense of short-term profits. Providing customer value in marketing networks Superior market positions depend on the organization's customer base, relations with suppliers and partners, relations with customers (e.g. brand equity), facilities and systems, and the organization's own endowment of technology and complementary property rights. These are the organization's assets or resource endowments which it has accumulated over time. In addition, the organization possesses certain capabilities, the glue that binds the organization's assets together and enables them to be used to advantage (Day 1994, p. 38). Capabilities are so deeply embedded in the organization's routines and practices that they cannot easily be traded or imitated (Dierickx and Cool 1989). The organization's competitive advantages are derived, therefore, from the nature of the its products, markets, technological orientation, resources and knowledge. Providing customer value means delivering on a whole range of promises to the customer. Products and services that customers perceive have a superior value compared to those of competitors are demanded while others are not, hence, the importance of the concept of 'value-added' defined as the component of customer value provided by an individual organization within the overall business system. Value is derived from the business system in which the organization operates. Each organization leverages other participants in the system – customers, suppliers and particularly others who complement the organization in what it provides – in creating that value (Figure 4.6). The value-added chain runs from suppliers through the organization forward to the customer aided by partners in the context of a competitive environment influenced by economic, political, legal and cultural factors. At each stage of the value chain there exists an opportunity to contribute positively to the organization's competitive strategy, by performing some activity or process in a way that is better than one's competitors, and so providing some uniqueness or advantage. If an organization attains such a competitive advantage which is sustainable,

Figure 4.6: Marketing System

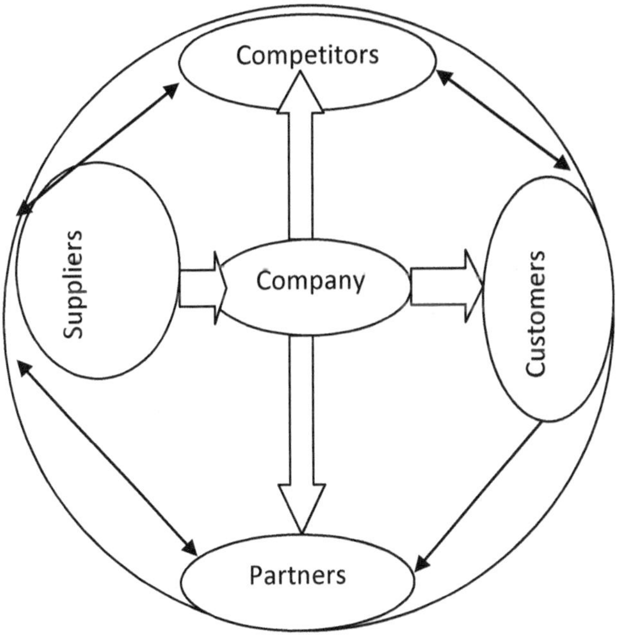

defensible, profitable and valued by the market, then it may earn high rates of return even though the industry structure may be unfavourable and the average profitability of the industry modest. A long-term marketing orientation draws together suppliers, customers, competitors and partners in the business system to create value in the marketing system. It is the business system as a whole that creates value. The marketing system consists of five major participant groups:

_ customers

_ competitors

_ partners

_ suppliers

_ the organization itself.

Viewing the value in the business system as the result of a network of important relationships highlights two important factors. First, decisions made by one organization affect and are affected by decisions by other organizations. Second, organizations often make decisions that are normally associated with those of other actors in the system. Thus, the organization makes important decisions which affect suppliers, just as suppliers make important decisions which are normally thought of as in the purview of the organization. Because so many decisions are part of a network in which a decision in one organization directly or indirectly influences decisions in other organizations, major decisions must be consistent with the goals of the participants in the network and their products. Herein lies the importance of the contribution of the leading organization – the organization making the key contribution to the establishment and growth of the business system (Moore 1993). This key contributor of value or the business system leader emerges in the early stage of the evolution of the business system to begin the process of continuous improvement which draws the entire business system towards an improved future.

A fundamental service provided by the business system leader is to encourage and persuade other organizations in the business system to complete the full value mix for customers by attracting 'follower' or 'imitator' organizations and thereby prevent them from developing other emerging business systems. The multitude of decisions in the business system must complement each other to maximize their overall positive impact on value. Within this framework the organization must decide its overall product–market business system strategy which has two elements – decisions on product–market segments and decisions on positions to adopt within the business system itself.

Figure 4.7: Generic Product-Market and Business System Strategies

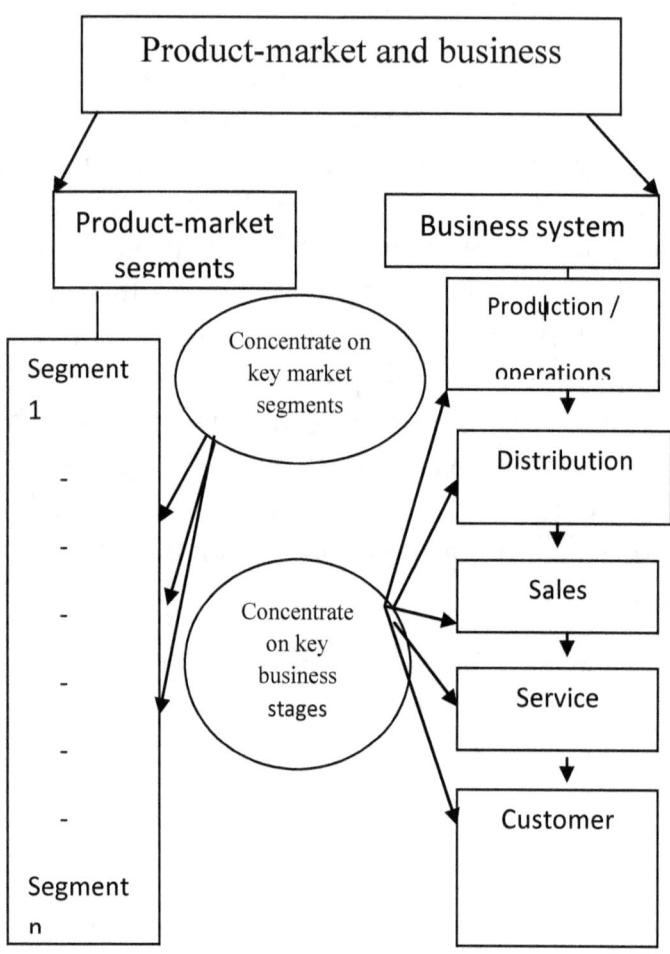

The organization's resource base enables it to decide the appropriate positions on which to focus in the business system.

Sources of Marketing Advantage

Sources of marketing advantage are reputation, brands, tangible assets, knowledge, customer service and people. To be worthwhile the marketing advantage must be sustainable. It must, therefore, be tangible, measurable and capable of providing competitive protection for some time. An illusory marketing advantage is one that is easily matched by competitors. The organization's marketing advantage depends on how well it chooses its strategy:

_ Concentrating on selected market segments.

_ Offering differentiated products.

_ Using alternative distribution channels.

_ Using different manufacturing processes to allow higher quality at lower prices.

Superior skills and resources, taken together, represent the ability of the organization to do more and better than its competitors. Superior skills are the distinctive capabilities of people in the organization that distinguish them from people in competing organizations, e.g. superior marketing skills that lead to fewer product failures in the marketplace or superior selling and distribution skills which lead to fewer returns of unwanted products and improved customer satisfaction.

Organizational Resources and Marketing Capabilities
Organizations are endowed with different amounts and types of resources and capabilities, which allow them to compete in different ways. Organizations which are better endowed have lower average costs than competitors and can provide products and services at lower cost or provide greater customer value. These resources are difficult to transfer among organizations because of transaction costs and because the assets may contain tacit knowledge (Teece *et al.* 1996, p. 15). Such resources and core capabilities of the organization, particularly those which involve collective learning and are knowledge based, are enhanced as they are applied (Prahalad and Hamel 1990). Resources and capabilities which are distinctive and superior, relative to those of rivals, may become the basis for competitive advantage if they are matched appropriately to market opportunities (Thompson Jr. and Strickland 1996, pp. 94–5). These resources may, therefore, provide both the basis and direction for the growth of the organization itself, i.e. there may be a natural trajectory embedded in a organization's knowledge base (Peteraf 1993, p. 182). Hence, the importance of studying the organization itself when attempting to predict its likely performance.

Resources and capabilities determine the organization's long-run strategy and are the primary source of profit. In an environment which is changing rapidly and where consumer tastes and preferences are volatile and myriad, a definition of the business in terms of what the organization is capable of doing may offer a more durable basis for strategy than a traditional definition, based solely on needs and wants of consumers. Defining markets too broadly is of little help to the organization that cannot easily develop the capabilities to serve such a broad market.

The organization's ability to earn profits depends on two factors:

_ the success of the organization in establishing competitive advantage over rivals; and

_ the attractiveness of the industry in which the organization competes.

As was seen above, the two sources of competitive advantage are:

_ the ability of the organization to reduce costs; and _ its ability to differentiate itself in ways that are important to customers.

The ability to establish a cost advantage requires the possession of scale efficient plants, access to low-cost raw materials or labour and superior process technology.

Figure 4.8: Influence of Resources on the Profitability of the Firm

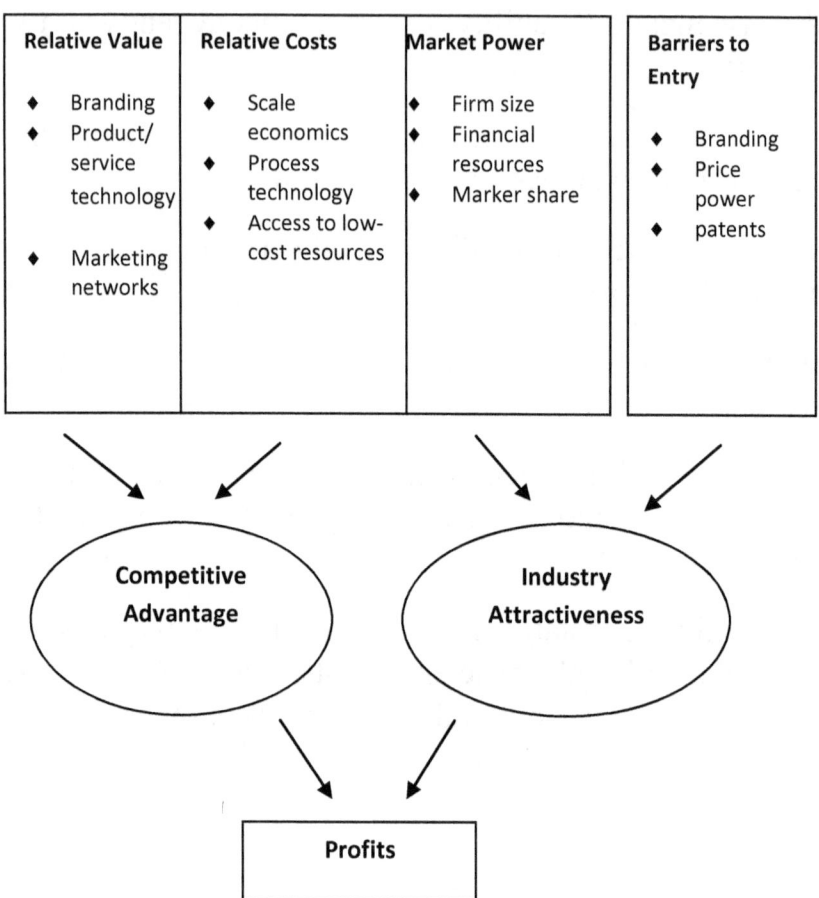

Differentiation advantages derive from brand reputation, proprietary and patented technology and an extensive marketing network covering distribution, sales and services. The attractiveness of an industry depends on the power the organization can exert over customers, rivals and others in the business system, which derives from the existence of market entry barriers.

Market entry barriers are based on brands, patents, price and the power of competitive retaliation. These are resources which are accumulated slowly over time and a new entrant can only obtain at disproportionate expense (Grant 1991, p. 115). Other sourcesof market power such as price-setting abilities depend on market share which is a consequence of cost efficiency, organization size and financial resources. Grant (1991) has integrated these ideas in a way which serves as a very convenient summary of this discussion (Figure 4.8).

Strategic Marketing Effectiveness Marketing's role in strategic planning for the organization means identifying the optimal long-term positions that will ensure customer satisfaction and support. These optimal positions are determined largely by fundamental changes in demographic, economic, social and political factors (Anderson 1982, p. 24). Thus, strategic positioning is more likely to be guided by long term demographic and socioeconomic research than by surveys of consumer attitudes, the hallmark of the market-driven organization. Value in marketing is a combination of product or service quality, reasonable or acceptable prices and responsive service. It is noteworthy that marketing value combines high quality with acceptable prices. It is not low quality products at low prices or high quality at high prices. Value in marketing means delivering on a whole range of promises to the customer.

Marketing effectiveness is not necessarily revealed by current marketing performance. Good results and growing sales may be due to the organization being in the right place at the right time rather than having effective marketing management. This is frequently the situation during the entrepreneurial phase of an organization's growth and development. The innovator frequently has considerable discretion in the market. At this stage the driving force is entrepreneurship rather than marketing. With acceptance of the product or service in the market and with the rise in competition which normally accompanies the acceptance of a new product or service, performance becomes more marketing-dependent. In a competitive environment, especially where customers have learned how to respond to various offerings, the situation changes. Improvements in marketing in the organization might improve results while another organization might have poor results in spite of excellent marketing planning. It depends on how well the organization matches its own resources against those of the competition to attract and hold the loyalty of customers.

The marketing effectiveness of the organization in serving customers in the face of existing and potential competition is reflected in the degree to which it exhibits five major attributes of a marketing orientation:

_ demonstrated customer philosophy

_ integrated marketing orientation

_ possesses adequate marketing information

_ adopts a strategic orientation

_ experiences a high level of operational efficiency.

The performance of the organization on these individual attributes may be used to indicate which elements of effective marketing action need most attention. It should be recognized, however, that this evaluation provides general information only but has the merit of obtaining an approximate measure of the orientation of the organization.

Key Marketing Success Factors
The organization attempts to convert skills and resources into superior market positions and thereby meet performance objectives. A knowledge of the key marketing success factors is essential to enable the organization to invest in markets and marketing to ensure performance objectives are attained. By identifying the key success factors the organization can identify ways of obtaining the greatest improvement in performance for the least expenditure. The key success factors of any business are the skills and resources which exert the highest degree of leverage on market positions and future performance. Having identified them, the organization attempts to selectively allocate resources towards these sources of leverage. The drivers of market position advantage are the high leverage skills and resources that contribute most to lowering costs to or creating value for customers.

Strategic Marketing Focus on Customers
Marketing means identifying values desired by customers, providing them in some way, communicating these values to customer groups and delivering the value. Customer values refer to those benefits focused on solving customer problems and not merely on the products and services themselves. The focus is on the customer and on solving problems faced by the customer. This is an integrated longer-term view of marketing

(Figure 4.9). Seeking value from the customer's perspective means building a long-term mutually profitable relationship with customers instead of trying to maximize profits on each transaction. An emphasis on relationships rather than individual transactions focuses on the customer as the profit centre, not the product. It also means that attracting new customers is an intermediate objective in the process of maintaining and cultivating an existing customer base. This interactive approach views marketing as a continuous relationship with customers in contrast to the more traditional and almost adversarial view which is short term and focused on immediate sales. The first sale to a customer is often very difficult, costs a lot and results in little or no profit. With a strong continuing relationship the customer becomes more profitable. Such long-term relationships are established through the exchange of information, products, services and social contacts. In this way the organization–customer relationship is commercialized.

The fundamental issue is to understand the customer's perception of value and to determine a superior value position from this perspective and to ensure that, by developing a consensus throughout the organization, that value is provided and communicated to the customer group in selected markets. The role of marketing in the business system is:

- To understand the customer's perception of value – identify the value the organization expects to provide.
- To determine a superior value position for the organization – provide the value expected.

- To determine the appropriate positioning and brand strategy – communicate the value.
- To distribute and price the product/service deliver the value to the customer.

References

Figure 4.9: Integrated Marketing Orientation

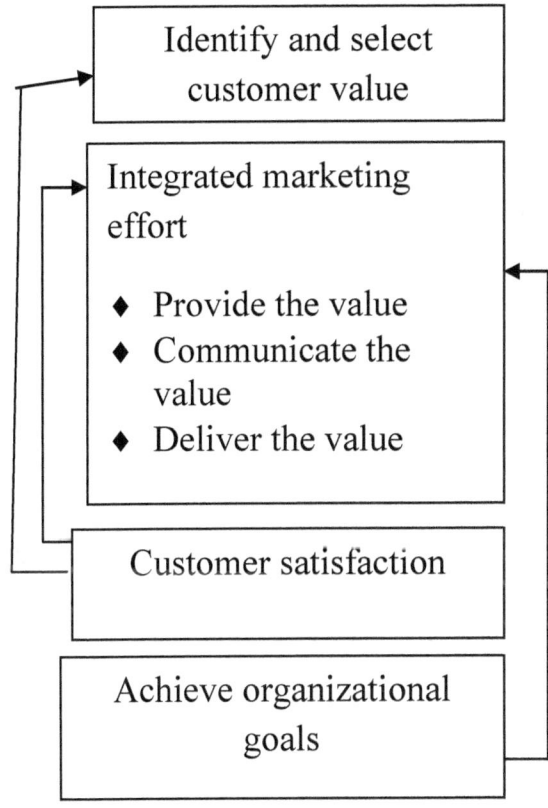

CHAPTER 5

STRATEGIC MARKETING PLANNING AND ENVIRONMENTAL ANALYSIS

Every Chief Executive Officer (CEO) or marketing executive periodically faces urgent strategic marketing challenges that can affect the future of the company for many years. Frequently these decisions are made without having an opportunity to study the situation and make the best possible decision. Making spur of the moment strategic decisions reduces the likelihood that these decisions are the best. A better approach is to perform an annual comprehensive review of markets and opportunities, then make long-term strategic decisions without the distractions of day-to-day marketing and sales activities. Daily decisions then fit into the company's overall strategic marketing goals. It's important for a strategic marketing planning process to look at the company from the customer's point of view by asking questions that have a long time horizon, such as:

- What needs or problems cause customers to consider buying from our company?
- What improvements in the customer's personal or business life can we enable or improve?
- Which customer market segments are attracted to our company or products?
- Which customer motivations or values lead people to decide to purchase our products?

- What changes or trends in our customer base are affecting their general interest or attraction to products like ours?

Strategic versus Tactical Marketing Plans

What makes a strategic marketing plan different from a more tactical marketing communications plan? The key difference is the focus on meshing overall customer situations with your overall company direction.

For business-to-business marketers, this means combining industry sector segmentation and product use with other factors related to purchase decisions. These include the purchase criteria and decision motivations that affect large, enterprise size purchases. For example, the trend toward increased use of outsourcing to both domestic and global vendors creates markets for those suppliers. However, those vendors need to have a strategic marketing vision in order to see these new markets early enough to take advantage of the opportunity. For consumer marketers, this means using geographic and demographic segmentation, as well as psychographic segmentation (i.e., values, attitudes, lifestyles), and product usage motivations. For example, the aging population bubble creates a general increase in demand for a wide range of products. It also creates market niches that are large enough to make product development and marketing worthwhile. The same shifts can also reduce demand for other products. These long term shifts in markets are frequently misinterpreted as short-term competitive pressures or fluctuations in the economy. Instead of increasing advertising or sales efforts, it might be better to abandon a declining market.

Without a strategic marketing plan a company could waste resources or miss an opportunity. What's the cost of missing an opportunity? Of course, it's impossible to know at the time the opportunity is missed, but years later it will become clear when a competitor opens a new factory or enters a new market -- and their revenue grows faster than their competitors. In other words, the annual cost of a strategic marketing plan review is miniscule compared to the revenue, market share, and profitability it can generate.

Developing the Strategic Marketing Plan

The strategic marketing plan process typically has three stages:

1. Segment the market
   - Geographic
   - Demographic
   - Psychographic
   - Behavior
2. Profile the market segments
   - Revenue potential
   - Market share potential
   - Profitability potential
3. Develop a market segment marketing strategy
   - Market leader or product line extension
   - Mass marketing or targeted marketing
   - Direct or indirect sales

Marketing Strategies and Strategic Marketing

After analyzing market segments, customer interests, and the purchase process, it's time to create the strategic marketing plan. The strategic marketing plan document usually includes:

- Situational Analysis - Where is the company now?
    a. Market Characteristics
    b. Key Success Factors
    c. Competition and Product Comparisons
    d. Technology Considerations
    e. Legal Environment
    f. Social Environment
    g. Problems and Opportunities
- Marketing Objectives - Where does management want the company to go?
    a. Product Profile
    b. Target Market
    c. Target Volume in Dollars and/or Units
- Marketing Strategies - What should the company do to achieve its objectives?
    a. Product Strategy
    b. Pricing Strategy
    c. Promotion Strategy
    d. Distribution Strategy
    e. Marketing Strategy Projection

How to Use a Strategic Marketing Plan

Once a company's executive team has approved the strategic marketing plan it's time to take the next step -- create the tactical marketing programmes and projects needed to implement the plan.

These tactical programmes usually include:

- Product Development Plan
- Marketing Communications Plan
- Sales Development Plan
- Customer Service Plan

Benefiting from a Strategic Marketing Plan

The top-down process of developing a strategic marketing plan helps insure that all tactical marketing programmes support the company's goals and objectives, as well as convey a consistent message to customers.

This approach improves company efficiency in all areas, which helps improve revenue and market share growth, and minimizes expenses -- all of which lead to higher profitability.

How Cliff Allen can help develop your strategic marketing plan

With over 25-years of strategic marketing experience, and helping companies implement both traditional and online marketing and sales programmes, Cliff Allen brings a valuable perspective to developing strategic marketing plans and programmes.

Cliff can lead your strategic planning team, or assist senior management, throughout the entire strategic marketing plan process. He can help you:

- Research customer attitudes toward your company, your product category, and your competition.
- Evaluate the attractiveness of potential target markets

Marketing Strategies and Strategic Marketing

- Determine the competitive strengths and weaknesses of your company and your competitors
- Develop marketing communications and sales development strategies for each target market
- Design the metrics to measure performance

Marketing Plan and Business Plan

The terms marketing plan and business plan are frequently used in marketing literature. Quite often are they used in the same context and it might be confusing to understand what each plan comprises. Here follows an overview to clarify the differences between a marketing plan and a business plan. A business plan should precisely define a company's business; identify the goals and serves as a summary. The basic components include a current and pro forma balance sheet, an income statement and a cash flow analysis. A business plan helps the company to allocate resources properly, handle unforeseen complications and make good business decisions. A good business plan can be used for loan applications and serves a purpose as information for customers, suppliers and other stakeholders about the company's operations and goals. A business plan has, excluding the marketing plan, a mission statement, vision, an identification of competitors, location, purchasing strategies and human resources.

A marketing plan is made in addition to a business plan and helps the management set realistic short, medium and long-term objectives for the marketing. It should help the company to focus on the most important areas of marketing and to have the right information or data to manage the marketing efforts.

There are two major components to your marketing strategy:

- how your enterprise will address the competitive marketplace
- how you will implement and support your day to day operations.

In today's very competitive marketplace a strategy that insures a consistent approach to offering your product or service in a way that will outsell the competition is critical. However, in concert with defining the marketing strategy you must also have a well defined methodology for the day to day process of implementing it. It is of little value to have a strategy if you lack either the resources or the expertise to implement it.

In the process of creating a marketing strategy you must consider many factors. Of those many factors, some are more important than others. Because each strategy must address some unique considerations, it is not reasonable to identify 'every' important factor at a generic level. However, many are common to all marketing strategies. Some of the more critical are described below:

You begin the creation of your strategy by deciding what the overall objective of your enterprise should be. In general this falls into one of four categories:

- If the market is very attractive and your enterprise is one of the strongest in the industry you will want

to invest your best resources in support of your offering.
- If the market is very attractive but your enterprise is one of the weaker ones in the industry you must concentrate on strengthening the enterprise, using your offering as a stepping stone toward this objective.
- If the market is not especially attractive, but your enterprise is one of the strongest in the industry then an effective marketing and sales effort for your offering will be good for generating near term profits.
- If the market is not especially attractive and your enterprise is one of the weaker ones in the industry you should promote this offering only if it supports a more profitable part of your business (for instance, if this segment completes a product line range) or if it absorbs some of the overhead costs of a more profitable segment. Otherwise, you should determine the most cost effective way to divest your enterprise of this offering.

The Product/Service - Factors for Consideration

You should be thoroughly familiar with the factors that establish products/services as strong contenders in the marketplace. Factors to consider include:

- Whether some or all of the technology for the offering is proprietary to the enterprise.
- The benefits the prospect will derive from use of the offering.

- The extent to which the offering is differentiated from the competition.
- The extent to which common introduction problems can be avoided such as lack of adherence to industry standards, unavailability of materials, poor quality control, regulatory problems and the inability to explain the benefits of the offering to the prospect.
- The potential for product obsolescence as affected by the enterprise's commitment to product development, the product's proximity to physical limits, the ongoing potential for product improvements, the ability of the enterprise to react to technological change and the likelihood of substitute solutions to the prospect's needs.
- Impact on customer's business as measured by costs of trying out your offering, how quickly the customer can realize a return from their investment in your offering, how disruptive the introduction of your offering is to the customer's operations and the costs to switch to your offering.
- The complexity of your offering as measured by the existence of standard interfaces, difficulty of installation, number of options, requirement for support devices, training and technical support and the requirement for complementary product interface.

Generic Marketing Strategies

Having selected the direction most beneficial for the overall interests of the enterprise, the next step is to choose a strategy for the offering that will be most effective in the market. This means choosing one of the following 'generic' strategies (first described by Michael Porter in his work, Competitive Advantage).

- A Cost Leadership Strategy is based on the concept that you can produce and market a good quality product or service at a lower cost than your competitors. These low costs should translate to profit margins that are higher than the industry average. Some of the conditions that should exist to support a cost leadership strategy include an on-going availability of operating capital, good process engineering skills, close management of labor, products designed for ease of manufacturing and low cost distribution.
- A Differentiation Strategy is one of creating a product or service that is perceived as being unique "throughout the industry". The emphasis can be on brand image, proprietary technology, special features, superior service, a strong distributor network or other aspects that might be specific to your industry. This uniqueness should also translate to profit margins that are higher than the industry average. In addition, some of the conditions that should exist to support a differentiation strategy include strong marketing abilities, effective product engineering, creative personnel, the ability to perform basic research and a good reputation.
- A Focus Strategy may be the most sophisticated of the generic strategies, in that it is a more 'intense' form of either the cost leadership or differentiation strategy. It is designed to address a "focused"

segment of the marketplace, product form or cost management process and is usually employed when it isn't appropriate to attempt an 'across the board' application of cost leadership or differentiation. It is based on the concept of serving a particular target in such an exceptional manner, that others cannot compete. Usually this means addressing a substantially smaller market segment than others in the industry, but because of minimal competition, profit margins can be very high.

Pricing - Operational Strategies

Having defined the overall offering objective and selecting the generic strategy you must then decide on a variety of closely related operational strategies. One of these is how you will price the offering. A pricing strategy is mostly influenced by your requirement for net income and your objectives for long term market control. There are three basic strategies you can consider.

- A Skimming Strategy

If your offering has enough differentiation to justify a high price and you desire quick cash and have minimal desires for significant market penetration and control, then you set your prices very high.

- A Market Penetration Strategy

If near term income is not so critical and rapid market penetration for eventual market control is desired, then you set your prices very low.

Marketing Strategies and Strategic Marketing

A Comparable Pricing Strategy

If you are not the market leader in your industry then the leaders will most likely

- have created a 'price expectation' in the minds of the marketplace. In this case you can price your offering comparably to those of your competitors.

Promotion - Operational Strategies

To sell an offering you must effectively promote and advertise it. There are two basic promotion strategies, PUSH and PULL.

- The Push Strategy maximizes the use of all available channels of distribution to "push" the offering into the marketplace. This usually requires generous discounts to achieve the objective of giving the channels incentive to promote the offering, thus minimizing your need for advertising.
- The Pull Strategy requires direct interface with the end user of the offering. Use of channels of distribution is minimized during the first stages of promotion and a major commitment to advertising is required. The objective is to "pull" the prospects into the various channel outlets creating a demand the channels cannot ignore.

There are many strategies for advertising an offering. Some of these include:

- Product Comparison advertising

In a market where your offering is one of several providing similar capabilities, if your offering stacks up well when comparing features then a product comparison ad can be beneficial.

- Product Benefits advertising

When you want to promote your offering without comparison to competitors, the product benefits ad is the correct approach. This is especially beneficial when you have introduced a new approach to solving a user need and comparison to the old approaches is inappropriate.

- Product Family advertising

If your offering is part of a group or family of offerings that can be of benefit to the customer as a set, then the product family ad can be of benefit.

- Corporate advertising

    When you have a variety of offerings and your audience is fairly broad, it is often beneficial to promote your enterprise identity rather than a specific offering.

Distribution - Operational Strategies

You must also select the distribution method(s) you will use to get the offering into the hands of the customer. These include:

- On-premise Sales involves the sale of your offering using a field sales organization that visits the prospect's facilities to make the sale.
- Direct Sales involves the sale of your offering using a direct, in-house sales organization that does all selling through the Internet, telephone or mail order contact.
- Wholesale Sales involves the sale of your offering using intermediaries or "middle-men" to distribute your product or service to the retailers.
- Self-service Retail Sales involves the sale of your offering using self service retail methods of distribution.
- Full-service Retail Sales involves the sale of your offering through a full service retail distribution channel.

Of course, making a decision about pricing, promotion and distribution is heavily influenced by some key factors in the industry and marketplace. These factors should be analyzed initially to create the strategy and then regularly monitored for changes. If any of them change substantially the strategy should be reevaluated.

The Environment

Environmental factors positively or negatively impact the industry and the market growth potential of your product/service. Factors to consider include:

- Government actions - Government actions (current or under consideration) can support or detract from your strategy. Consider subsidies, safety, efficacy

and operational regulations, licensing requirements, materials access restrictions and price controls.
- Demographic changes - Anticipated demographic changes may support or negatively impact the growth potential of your industry and market. This includes factors such as education, age, income and geographic location.
- Emerging technology - Technological changes that are occurring may or may not favor the actions of your enterprise.
- Cultural trends - Cultural changes such as fashion trends and life style trends may or may not support your offering's penetration of the market

Macro Environment

Macro environment is defined as uncontrollable factors that constitute the external environment of marketing including demographic, economic, technological, natural, socio-cultural, and regulatory forces; the general external business environment which an organisation is active in. The macro environment is generally divided into four areas, which are investigated with a PEST-analysis.

PEST-analysis

A PEST-analysis is the identification of the *political, economic, social and technological* influences on an organisation. The macro environment cannot be managed but it is necessary to take the factors into consideration while developing a strategy. It is an analysis of the macro environment and topics affecting environmental factors and their importance should be investigated in the macro

Marketing Strategies and Strategic Marketing environment analysis.

Table 5.1: A PEST- Analysis of Environmental Influences

Political/Legal	Economic factors
• Monopolies legislation • Environmental protection laws • Taxation policy • Foreign trade regulations • Employment law • Government stability • Political situation	• Business cycles • GNP trends • Interest rates • Money supply • Inflation • Unemployment • Disposable income • Energy availability and cost • Balance of Payments • Exchange rate
Socio-cultural factors	Technological
• Population demographics • Income distribution	• Government spending on research • Government and industry focus on technological

• Social mobility • Lifestyle changes • Attitudes to work and leisure • Consumerism • Levels of education • Suppliers • Competitors • Cost of Raw materials • Product / Service Life Cycle • Cost of labour	effort • New discoveries / development • Speed of technology transfer • Rates of obsolescence

A PEST-analysis of environmental influences (p 105, Johnson, G, Scholes, K, *Exploring Corporate Strategy*, 1999)

The Prospect

It is essential to understand the market segment(s) as defined by the prospect characteristics you have selected as the target for your offering. Factors to consider include:

- The potential for market penetration involves whether you are selling to past customers or a new prospect, how aware the prospects are of what you are offering, competition, growth rate of the industry and demographics.
- The prospect's willingness to pay higher price because your offering provides a better solution to their problem.
- The amount of time it will take the prospect to make a purchase decision is affected by the prospects confidence in your offering, the number and quality of competitive offerings, the number of people involved in the decision, the urgency of the need for your offering and the risk involved in making the purchase decision.
- The prospect's willingness to pay for product value is determined by their knowledge of competitive pricing, their ability to pay and their need for characteristics such as quality, durability, reliability, ease of use, uniformity and dependability.
- Likelihood of adoption by the prospect is based on the criticality of the prospect's need, their attitude about change, the significance of the benefits, barriers that exist to incorporating the offering into daily usage and the credibility of the offering.

The Competition

It is essential to know who the competition is and to understand their strengths and weaknesses. Factors to consider include:

- Each of your competitor's experience, staying power, market position, strength, predictability and freedom to abandon the market must be evaluated.

Your Enterprise

An honest appraisal of the strength of your enterprise is a critical factor in the development of your strategy. Factors to consider include:

- Enterprise capacity to be leader in low-cost production considering cost control infrastructure, cost of materials, economies of scale, management skills, availability of personnel and compatibility of manufacturing resources with offering requirements.
- The enterprise's ability to construct entry barriers to competition such as the creation of high switching costs, gaining substantial benefit from economies of scale, exclusive access to or clogging of distribution channels and the ability to clearly differentiate your offering from the competition.
- The enterprise's ability to sustain its market position is determined by the potential for competitive imitation, resistance to inflation, ability to maintain high prices, the potential for product obsolescence and the 'learning curve' faced by the prospect.
- The prominence of the enterprise.
- The competence of the management team.
- The adequacy of the enterprise's infrastructure in terms of organization, recruiting capabilities,

employee benefit programmes, customer support facilities and logistical capabilities.
- The freedom of the enterprise to make critical business decisions without undue influence from distributors, suppliers, unions, creditors, investors and other outside influences.
- Freedom from having to deal with legal problems.

Development
A review of the strength and viability of the product/service development programme will heavily influence the direction of your strategy. Factors to consider include:

- The strength of the development manager including experience with personnel management, current and new technologies, complex projects and the equipment and tools used by the development personnel.
- Personnel who understand the relevant technologies and are able to perform the tasks necessary to meet the development objectives.
- Adequacy and appropriateness of the development tools and equipment.
- The necessary funding to achieve the development objectives.
- Design specifications that are manageable.

Production
You should review your enterprise's production organization with respect to their ability to cost effectively produce products/services. The following factors are considered:

- The strength of production manager including experience with personnel management, current and new technologies, complex projects and the equipment and tools used by the manufacturing personnel.
- Economies of scale allowing the sharing of operations, sharing of production and the potential for vertical integration.
- Technology and production experience
- The necessary production personnel skill level and/or the enterprise's ability to hire or train qualified personnel.
- The ability of the enterprise to limit suppliers bargaining power.
- The ability of the enterprise to control the quality of raw materials and production.
- Adequate access to raw materials and sub-assembly production.

Marketing/Sales

The marketing and sales organization is analyzed for its strengths and current activities. Factors to consider include:

- Experience of Marketing/Sales manager including contacts in the industry (prospects, distribution channels, media), familiarity with advertising and promotion, personal selling capabilities, general management skills and a history of profit and loss responsibilities.
- The ability to generate good publicity as measured by past successes, contacts in the press, quality of

promotional literature and market education capabilities.
- Sales promotion techniques such as trade allowances, special pricing and contests.
- The effectiveness of your distribution channels as measured by history of relations, the extent of channel utilization, financial stability, reputation, access to prospects and familiarity with your offering.
- Advertising capabilities including media relationships, advertising budget, past experience, how easily the offering can be advertised and commitment to advertising.
- Sales capabilities including availability of personnel, quality of personnel, location of sales outlets, ability to generate sales leads, relationship with distributors, ability to demonstrate the benefits of the offering and necessary sales support capabilities.
- The appropriateness of the pricing of your offering as it relates to competition, price sensitivity of the prospect, prospect's familiarity with the offering and the current market life cycle stage.

Market Opportunities

Opportunities in the business environment are those factors that provide possibilities for a business to expand and increase sales and profits. A successful company identify the threats and eliminate them or turn them into opportunities.

Market Segments

High development costs as well as competitive pressures are forcing companies to rush products into as many markets as possible. But at the same time, a company can ill afford new products that are not effectively introduced, marketed, and supported in each market the company competes in. A balance must be found and a first step is to identify interesting market segments.

Targeting

The focus should be put on the market segment that has the most opportunities for the company. Characteristics of the intended target market must be identified and dealt with. The main characteristics can be summarised by eight O:s, occupants, objects, occasions, objectives, outlets, organisation, operations and opposition. Occupants are targets of the marketing effort and should be categorised in different dimensions such as demographics, geography, psychographics or product-related variables (usage rate and brand loyalty for example). Occasions are moments when members of the target market buy the product or service and the objectives are the motives behind the purchase. A computer software provider markets not products but solutions to problems.

Outlets are places where customers expect to be able to procure a product or be exposed to messages about it. The organisation describes how the buying or acceptance of an idea takes place. It is interesting to know who makes the decisions in an organisation and how the operations behind the purchase request proceed. The opposition refers to the competition in the market segment and that will vary from direct product-type competition to competition from other products that satisfy same need.

Customer Services

The strength of the customer service function has a strong influence on long term market success. Factors to consider include:

- Experience of the Customer Service manager in the areas of similar offerings and customers, quality control, technical support, product documentation, sales and marketing.
- The availability of technical support to service your offering after it is purchased.
- One or more factors that causes your customer support to stand out as unique in the eyes of the customer.
- Accessibility of service outlets for the customer.
- The reputation of the enterprise for customer service.

After defining your strategy you must use the information you have gathered to determine whether this strategy will achieve the objective of making your enterprise competitive in the marketplace.

Cost to Enter Market

This is an analysis of the factors that will influence your costs to achieve significant market penetration. Factors to consider include:

- Your marketing strength.

- Access to low cost materials and effective production.
- The experience of your enterprise.
- The complexity of introduction problems such as lack of adherence to industry standards, unavailability of materials, poor quality control, regulatory problems and the inability to explain the benefits of the offering to the prospect.
- The effectiveness of the enterprise infrastructure in terms of organization, recruiting capabilities, employee benefit programmes, customer support facilities and logistical capabilities.
- Distribution effectiveness as measured by history of relations, the extent of channel utilization, financial stability, reputation, access to prospects and familiarity with your offering.
- Technological efforts likely to be successful as measured by the strength of the development organization.
- The availability of adequate operating capital.

Profit Potential

This is an analysis of the factors that could influence the potential for generating and maintaining profits over an extended period. Factors to consider include:

- Potential for competitive retaliation is based on the competitors resources, commitment to the industry, cash position and predictability as well as the status of the market.
- The enterprise's ability to construct entry barriers to competition such as the creation of high switching costs, gaining substantial benefit from

Marketing Strategies and Strategic Marketing

economies of scale, exclusive access to or clogging of distribution channels and the ability to clearly differentiate your offering from the competition.
- The intensity of competitive rivalry as measured by the size and number of competitors, limitations on exiting the market, differentiation between offerings and the rapidity of market growth.
- The ability of the enterprise to limit suppliers bargaining power.
- The enterprise's ability to sustain its market position is determined by the potential for competitive imitation, resistance to inflation, ability to maintain high prices, the potential for product obsolescence and the 'learning curve' faced by the prospect.
- The availability of substitute solutions to the prospect's need.
- The prospect's bargaining power as measured by the ease of switching to an alternative, the cost to look at alternatives, the cost of the offering, the differentiation between your offering and the competition and the degree of the prospect's need.
- Market potential for new products considering market growth, prospect's need for your offering, the benefits of the offering, the number of barriers to immediate use, the credibility of the offering and the impact on the customer's daily operations. The freedom of the enterprise to make critical business decisions without undue influence from distributors, suppliers, unions, investors and other outside influences.

Action Plan

In the action plan are the activities to be able to reach the marketing objectives listed. An action plan should be written and the plan should include details of the tactics for reaching the objectives. The activities are divided into four groups, product, pricing, distribution and promotion activities.

Control

The control is used to assess effectiveness of strategies and actions and to modify strategies and actions if necessary. The objective states where the company wants to be and the plan how it should act to reach it. The control should monitor the proposed plans as they proceed.

Figure 5.1: The Marketing Control Process

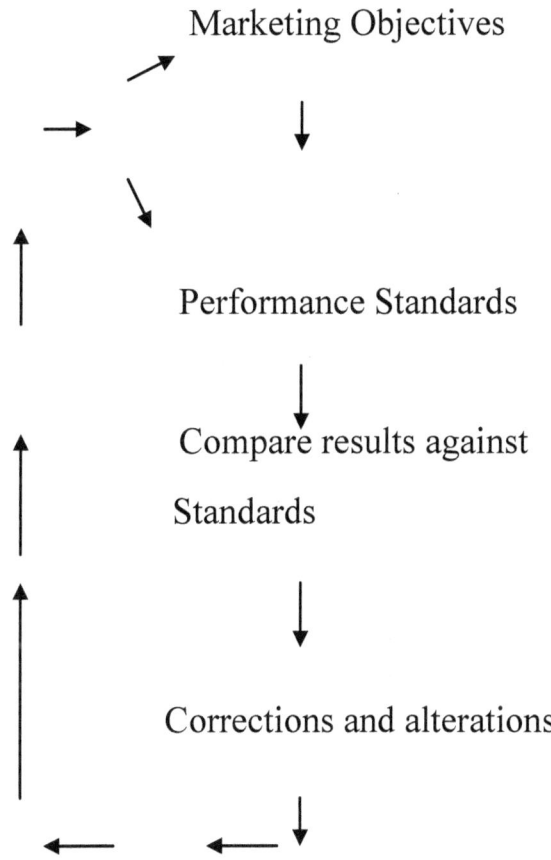

Control involves measurement, evaluation, and monitoring. Resources are scarce and costly so it is important to control marketing plans. Assuming from the marketing objectives are performance standards set and the actual progress will be compared to these. These standards can be completion dates or sales objectives for different activities. Corrective action (if any) is then taken. If corrective action is taken, an investigation also needs to be undertaken to establish precisely why the difference occurred. The marketing plan can be controlled in many ways, for example through market share analysis, sales analysis, quality controls and cash flow statements.

Product Launch Strategy
A typical activity in an action plan is a product launch. The impact of an effective product launch can be great, but so can the cost of one that is poorly executed. For software products is it common to do a global product launch. That means introducing a product into countries in more regions within a narrow time frame. To achieve this, a company must undertake a number of measures. The company should be involved in the first stage of the product strategy formulation to ensure that local and regional considerations are part of the overall corporate and product messages. A product launch team consisting of representatives from different departments can approach problems from an industry standpoint, as opposed to a home country perspective, enhancing product competitiveness in all markets. Adequate consideration should be given to localisation and translation requirements before the launch. The advantage of a simultaneous launch is that it boosts the overall momentum and attractiveness of the product by making it immediately available in key geographic markets. Global product launches require more education and support of the sales channel than domestic efforts or drawn-out efforts do. This is due to the

diversity of the distribution channels in terms of support and education they may require before the launch. A successfully executed global launch offers several benefits. It permits the company to showcase its technology in all major markets at the same time. By setting a single date for the launch, the entire organisation will be forced to gear up quickly for a successful worldwide effort. A simultaneous worldwide introduction also solves the dilemma of having old models or versions in some markets while customers know of the existence of the new product. (Czinkota, M, Ronkainen, I, 2001).

Multi-Product Resource Allocation Having the product on the market allows the validation or rejection of important estimates or assumptions about customer attitudes and behavior that would have been made during the development-phase. It could also reveal unanticipated problems or opportunities. The company can now get to know if the customers find problems in using the product, if they use it as much as expected and the satisfaction of the customers. The product launch should be evaluated and that can be done in the three areas product platform evolution and brand extensions, market evolution and competitive evolution. Companies and organisations that use software are in general very good at following trends and news in their own area. Software companies should have informative and technologic advanced web sites because of software companies' high demand and expectation in the computer science's area. To find the right time for a product launch many factors need to be taken into consideration. It is important to coordinate the launch with competitors' launches of almost the same products. Launching a similar product as a competitor did two weeks earlier is not only pointless it is also waste of money.

The most common resource allocation methods are:

- Percentage of sales
- Executive judgment
- All-you-can-afford
- Match competitors
- Last year based

Another method is called decision calculus. Managers are asked four questions:

What would sales be with:

1. no sales force
2. half the current effort
3. 50% greater effort
4. a saturation level of effort.

From these answers, one can determine the parameters of the S-curve response function and use linear programmeming techniques to determine resource allocations.

Decision algorithms that result in extreme solutions, such as allocating most of the sales force to one product while neglecting another product often do not yield practical solutions.

For mature products, sales increase very little as a function of advertising expenditures. For newer products however, there is a very positive correlation.

Portfolio models may be used to allocate resources among major product lines or business units. The BCG growth-share matrix is one such model.

New Product Diffusion Curve

As a new product diffuses into the market, some types of consumers such as innovators and early adopters buy the product before other consumers. The product adoption follows a trajectory that is shaped like a bell curve and is known as the product diffusion curve. The marketing strategy should take this adoption curve into account and address factors that influence the rate of adoption by the different types of consumers.

Dynamic Product Management Strategies

Two fundamental issues of product management are whether to pioneer or follow, and how to manage the product over its life cycle.

Order of market entry is very important. In fact, the forecasted market share relative to the pioneering brand is the pioneering brand's share divided by the square root of the order of entry. For example, the brand that entered third is forecasted to have $1/\sqrt{3}$ times the market share of the first entrant (*Marketing Science*, Vol. 14, No. 3, Part 2 of 2, 1995.) This rule was determined empirically.

The pioneering advantage is obtained from both the supply and demand side. From the supply side, there are raw material advantages, better experience effects to provide a cost advantage, and channel pre-emption. On the demand side, there is the advantage of familiarity, the chance to set a standard, and the choice of perceptual position.

Once a firm gains a pioneering advantage, it can maintain it by improving the product, creating a standard, advertise that it was the first, and introduce a new product in the market that may cannibalize the first but deter other firms from entering.

There also are disadvantages to being the pioneer. Being first allows a competitor to leapfrog the early technology. The incumbent develops inertia in its R&D and may not be a flexible as newcomers. Developing an industry has costs that the pioneer must bear alone, and the way the industry develops and its potential size are not deterministic.

There are four classic price/selling effort strategies as shown in table 5.1:

Table 5.1: Selling Effort

Selling Effort	Price	
	Low	High
Low	Necessity Goods	Classic Skim Strategy Vulnerable to new entrants
High	Classic Penetration Strategy	Luxury Goods

In general, products are clustered in the low-low or high-high categories. If a product is in a mixed category, after introduction it will tend to move to the low-low or high-high one.

Increasing the breadth of the product line as several advantages; a firm can better serve multiple segments, it can occupy more of the distributors' shelf space, it offers customers a more complete selection, and it pre-empts competition. While a wider range of products will cause a firm to cannibalize some of its own sales, it is better to do so oneself rather than let the competition do so.

The drawbacks of broad product lines are reduced volume for each brand (cannibalization), greater manufacturing complexity, increased inventory, more management resources required, more advertising (or less per brand), clutter and confusion in advertising for both customers and distributors.

To increase profits from existing brands, a firm can improve its production efficiency, increase the demand through more users, more uses, and more usage. A firm also can defend its existing base through line extensions (expand on a current brand), flanker brands (new brands in an existing product area), and brand extensions.

A SWOT ANALYSIS

Different techniques for analysis of resources and competences probably only give small separate parts, but with help from a SWOT analysis the parts are brought together to an overall picture of the market. SWOT stands for *s*trengths, *w*eaknesses, *o*pportunities and *t*hreats and summarises the key issues from an analysis of the business environment and the strategic capabilities of an organisation. The strengths and weaknesses identify the internal situation in the company and the opportunities and threats identify the external situation. This is undertaken together with micro- and macro environmental analyses.

The idea is not only to list these variables of manager's perception; rather to undertake a more structured analysis concerning them. A structured SWOT-analysis is an important tool for the formulation of the organisation's strategy. It can be used to assess whether there are opportunities to exploit further, for example the unique resources or core competences of the organisation. The goal is to identify the extent to which the current strategy of an organisation and its more specific strengths and weaknesses are relevant to, and capable of, dealing with the changes taking place in the business environment. (Johnson, and Scholes, 1999). A factor can be both a threat and an opportunity, depending on how the organization works with the issue.

A SWOT analysis is a tool, used in management and strategy formulation. It can help to identify the Strengths, Weaknesses, Opportunities and Threats of a particular company.

Strengths and weaknesses are internal factors that create value or destroy value. They can include assets, skills, or resources that a company has at its disposal, compared to its competitors. They can be measured using internal assessments or external benchmarking.

Opportunities and threats are external factors that create value or destroy value. A company cannot control them. But they emerge from either the competitive dynamics of the industry/market or from demographic, economic, political, technical, social, legal or cultural factors (PEST). Typical examples of factors in a SWOT Analysis diagram shown in table 5.2:

Table 5.2: Factors in a SWOT Analysis

Strengths	Weaknesses
♦ Specialist marketing expertise ♦ Exclusive access to natural resources ♦ Patents ♦ New, innovative product or service ♦ Location of your business ♦ Cost advantage through proprietary know-how ♦ Quality processes and procedures ♦ Strong brand or reputation	♦ Lack of marketing expertise ♦ Undifferen-tiated products and service (i.e. in relation to your competitors) ♦ Location of your company ♦ Competitors have superior access to distribution channels ♦ Poor quality of goods or services ♦ Damaged reputation
Opportunities	**Threats**
♦ Developing market ♦ Mergers, joint ventures or strategic alliances ♦ Moving into new attractive market segments ♦ A new international market ♦ Loosening of regulations ♦ Removal	♦ A new competitor in your own home market ♦ Price war ♦ Competitor has a new, innovative substitute product or service ♦ New regulations ♦ Increased trade barriers

of international trade barriers ♦ A market that is led by a weak competitor	♦ A potential new taxation on your product or service

Any organization must try to create a fit with its external environment. The SWOT diagram is a very good tool for analyzing the (internal) strengths and weaknesses of a corporation and the (external) opportunities and threats. However, this analysis is just the first step. To really create the fit with the external environment is often the most difficult work.

Confrontation Matrix

A tool to combine the internal factors with the external factors is the Confrontation Matrix.

Table 5.3: Confrontation Matrix

	Opportunities	Threats
Strengths	Offensive make the most of these	Adjust Restore strengths
Weaknesses	Defensive watch competition closely	Survive Turn around

Often in reality the two columns of the SWOT diagram are pointing in opposite directions. Strategists must still deal with the paradox of creating alignment. This can be done via Outside-in strategy formulation (market-driven strategy) or Inside-out strategy formulation (resource-driven).

Note: you can also apply a SWOT analysis to competitors, often providing interesting new perspectives.

Comments on Uses of SWOT

| SWOT Absolutely essential | - This is the most important tool companies around the globe will need to survive and grow in our current uncertain economic climate. |

Marketing Strategies and Strategic Marketing

What is SWOT analysis?	A SWOT analysis is like showing a mirror to oneself. It tells where the person stands. Strength: gives power. One should analyse his Weakness. Opportunities should be grabbed and one should overcome his Threats.
SWOT Process Steps	Here's a list of typical phases in a medium size SWOT process (modify as needed by Fred Moran - USA 1. Determine clear objective(s) 2. Determine SWOT team (size, level, find good facilitator and contributors (mix of experts and creative people) 3. Gather Information / Research (who does what) 4. Prepare SWOT workshop (timing, find a suitable room, create a free open atmosphere, agenda with times, send invitations) 5. Workshop - Brainstorm and list the Strengths 6. Workshop - Brainstorm and list the Weaknesses 7. Workshop - Brainstorm and list the Opportunities 8. Workshop - Brainstorm and list the Threats 9. Workshop - Evaluate and Prioritize (use objectives) 10. Communicate the Results

11. Implement the Results

12. Monitor the Results"

Uses of SWOT analysis	A SWOT analysis is frequently used in an early stage of strategic or marketing planning for decision-making, problem solving, and as a tool to increase the awareness of certain people about the situation the firm is in. But you can also use SWOT as a personal career planning tool to assess and reflect upon your own personal Strengths, Weaknesses, Opportunities and Threats. Likewise, within the personnel department we can use SWOT to assess candidates for a function. You can even perform a SWOT on your football or hockey team...
SWOT Strengths and VRIO test	In order to analyze true, valid strengths in a SWOT Analysis, you can use the VRIO test: VALUE - Does the strength generate efficiency or more effectiveness? RARE - Is the strength also possessed by many competitors? IMITABILITY - Hard to copy / imitate? ORGANIZATIONAL - Can it be exploited by this organization?"

Opportunity or Threat?
There can be considerable debate about what is a threat and what is an

Marketing Strategies and Strategic Marketing

opportunity. When a company spots a new trend early and acts upon it well, then it has an opportunity. If another company does not see the same trend coming, or fails to act upon it well, then it is facing a threat. Furthermore, people with an entrepreneurial or can-do mentality view almost anything as an opportunity, while pessimistic, bureaucratic people view almost anything as a threat.

SWOT as a tool It is a popular experience that the SWOT analysis as a standalone tool is not better than a simple brainstorming process focused on the four different issues. In order to make it work, it is necessary to work several other analysis e.g. value chain analysis, competitor analysis, PEST analysis, Porters five forces, financial analysis etc before you can determine if you have a solid case. Otherwise you don't have any kind of proof to support why you think that your technology for instance is superior to your competitors, or that lack of size is a threat in the global competition. Only after you have done the initial work, you will be able to harvest the real value of the SWOT and if you decide to go a step further the TOWS matrix

(=confrontation matrix).

SWOT research is important	**SWOT** - A SWOT analysis can only be effectively executed if detailed and proper research work has been carried out. With detailed research you won't be groping in the dark, you have a comprehensive concept of both the internal and external factors and how to creatively and innovatively develop a strategy that is directional, cost effective and of course executable.
SWOT Considerations	Couple points to consider--first and foremost focus the SWOT as much as possible on the work to be done or the mission to be accomplished. The sharper the focus, the more meaningful the analysis outcome. Each data input should be rated - Information Confidence Level (1 = low confidence to 10 = high confidence). How confident are you that the information is valid and true (Objective / Subjective)? Finally, use SWOT analysis over time to look at "trends".

CHAPTER 6
MARKETING STRATEGY

In an organisation's environment, survival is often a continuous preoccupation of top management. In the game of survival various alternative strategies are possible. Various strategic options that can help firms survive in business environment are considered in this section. Conventional Business Strategies: Successful management of any organisation requires extra efforts and critical conceptual skills on the part of the policy formulators and strategy executors. The management of organizations by top executives involves the determination of missions, objectives and the deployment of resources adaptively before overwhelming impact could be created. In essence, "Progressive organizations need to develop adaptive abilities that will enable them succeed in a turbulent environment" (Fubara, 1998 : 21). This is why it becomes necessary that survival prone organizations should have a broad programmeme of activity effectively developed to achieve objective – strategy. Strategy facilitates the accomplishment of objectives and organizational mission. According to Schewe (1987: 49) "strategy provides some guidelines for competitive warfare that will direct the actual activities of the organisation. It specifies series of maneuvers designed to obtain a particular result; it is a blue print for action". The benefits attainable from the effective use of strategies by organizations cannot easily be fathomed casually. The importance of strategy to the achievement of organizational objective has made

Chandler, (1962) to maintain that the determination of the basic long-term goals and objectives of an enterprise, and the adoption of courses of action and the allocation of resources necessary to carry out these goals constitute a meaningful strategy. Strategy is defined Waterman, Jr. (1982 : 71) as "a coherent set of actions aimed at gaining a sustainable advantage over competition, improving position vis-à-vis customers or allocating resources". For future-oriented approach and result inclined strategy, Newman et al, (1985:9) insist that organisations should design and implement their strategies thus:

- Design company strategy on the basis of continuous matching of (a) anticipated opportunities and problems in the industry with (b) distinctive company strengths and limitations.
- Amplify and clarify this strategy in policy, which serves as a more specific guide to executives in the various functional divisions of the company.
- When a diversified corporation is involved, plan for a balanced portfolio strategy covering the several business units (companies), and modify the strategies and policies of the business-units to fit into this consolidated plan.
- Setup an organisation to carry out the strategy and policy
- Guide the execution of the strategy and policy through the organisation. This calls for programmeming, activating and controlling the operations.

All effective strategy designs call for:

(1) The identification of the particular services – that is, the product – market domain – which the company will promote;
(2) Selection of basic resource conversion technology by which these services will be created-a technology that hopefully will give the company some differential advantage as a member of the industry.
(3) Determination of the major thrusts necessary to move the company from its present course to the desired one with this concept of its economic and social mission; and finally
(4) Establishing the Criteria and the standards that will be used to measure achievement. Newman et al (1985) insist that no strategy is complete without all four of these dimension being clarified.

Strategy concentrates on basic directions, major thrust and overriding priorities. Ansoff (1969) opines that strategy is clarified by thinking through the more detailed policy and other parameters that guide execution of strategy. Strategy and policy at both the business-unit and corporate levels, are carried out by an organisation. Unless this organisation is well designed for its tasks, the strategy, however sound, may lead to mediocre or haphazard results.

There are strategies and there are strategies that lead to organisational success if effectively adopted. A strategy that is good for company X may be harmful for organisation Y because of certain factors. No real formula exists for identifying the right or effective strategy but a few suggestion have been made by Nnedu (1996, p. 26) to help strategists or organization evaluate their strategies for better results; they include:

(i) The strategy should be profitable or lead to profitable outcomes

(ii) The strategy should show some consistency with both the internal and external environments of the organisation.

(iii) The strategy should be capable of providing guideline for effective management and decision making.

(iv) The strategy should be appropriate when considered in relationship with available resources

(v) The strategy should be capable of accomplishing the objectives of the organisation.

(vi) The strategy should involve an adequate degree of risks. If the strategy is too risky, the organisation may be gambling with its scarce resources.

(vii) The strategy should be timely and or involve an appropriate time horizon. The strategy should be implementable at the moment of the need and it should be possible to determine when the results of the strategy can be expected.

(viii) When implemented, the strategy should be able to work or produce the desired results

(ix) The strategy should provide competitive edge rather than being highly vulnerable to market and environmental threats.

(x) The strategy should be consistent with corporate resources and the philosophy of top management and therefore capable of receiving full commitment of corporate resources.

(xi) The strategy should provide other opportunities or be strategically fit.

Generic Strategies

Successful organisations engage in definite patterns of behaviour in their business environment in order to increase returns on investment. Several studies have discovered some identical factors that promote success in business. Certain strategies are almost always appropriate regardless of the situation. The best known of these strategies regarded as generic have been researched by Porter, (1980). Porter, (1980) suggests that firms can take three basic approaches or strategies in general circumstances to be successful in competition. They include:

(i) Low Cost Strategy or Overall Cost Leadership: A firm that uses this strategy generally has access to the most modern production processes or low-cost supply sources or usually high sales volume, which also leads to more efficient production (Schewe, 1987). With this strategy, the organization works hard to achieve the lowest production and distribution costs, so that it can price lower than its competitors and win a large market. Firms pursuing this strategy must be good at engineering, purchasing, manufacturing and physical distribution. Low cost relative to competitors becomes the target of this strategy. Though quality service and other areas cannot be ignored (Stanton, 1981 and Enyioko, 1999).

(ii) Differentiation Strategy: This strategy emphasizes the use of company's unique features such as brand, product quality, dependable service, durability or advanced technology (Kotler, 1994). Effective differentiation leads to 'positioning strategy. Competitive positioning requires the firm to develop a general idea of what kind of offer to make to the target customers in relation to competitors offer. In developing a positioning or differentiation strategy company must ask in what specific ways can it obtain a competitive advantage over others in the industry. In differentiation strategy the organization concentrates on achieving superior performance in an important customer benefit area valued by a large part of the market (Straw, 1998). Effective use of differentiation strategy involves a firm creating something perceived in the industry as being unique. The organisation cultivates those strengths that will give it a competitive advantage in one benefit or more. Differentiation defined by Kotler, (1994: 307) as "the act of designing a set of meaningful differences to distinguish the company's offer from competitors offer" is a very effective generic strategy. Treacy and Wiersema, (1993) distinguished three strategies that lead to successful differentiation and market leadership as:

    (a) Operational excellence: Providing customers with reliable products or services at competitive prices and easy availability

    (b) Customer intimacy: knowing customers intimately and being able to respond quickly to their specific and special needs.

    (c) Product/service leadership: offering customers innovative products/services that enhance the customer's utility and outperform competitors products.

They insist that a company can win by operating its business better, knowing its customers better and consistently making better product. Equally, Garvin (1987) highlighted on the use of differentiation strategy by tabulating the main characteristics/features under which products, services, personnel and images could be differentiated and strategically positioned. They are shown in table 6.1

Table 6.1: Differentiation Variables

Products	Service	Personnel	Image
Features	Delivery	Competence	Symbol
Performance	Installation	Courtesy	Media
Conformance	Customer	Credibility	Atmosphere
Durability	Training	Reliability	Events
Reliability	Consulting	Responsibility	
Reparability	Service	Communication	
Style	Repair		
Design	Miscellaneous		

Source: Adapted from Garvin (1987: 101)

(iii) Focus Strategy: In this strategy the company restricts it business to a small group of buyers or a smaller set of products/services. The organization focuses on one or more narrow market segments rather than going after large market. The firm gets to know the needs of these segments and pursues either cost leadership or a form of differentiation within the target market (Kotler, 1994).

(iv) Other Generic Strategies: several strategies have been recommended for firms in specific situation. In his own studies, Hemermesh, (1984) suggested three strategies that could be used for firms in stagnant industries; they are:

    (a)   They should identify, create and exploit growth segments in their industries

(b) They should emphasize product quality and product improvement.
(c) They should systematically and consistently improve the efficiency of their production and distribution system.

Firms in the declining industries according to Harrigan (1980) must apply any of the following generic strategies

(a) Increasing investments: Increase investment only where this creates a long term advantage
(b) Milking the investment: Remove all possible cash flows
(c) Employing holding patterns: Hold your own
(d) Shrinking selectively: choose the available remaining markets and advance unto them strongly.
(e) Early exit: Getting out while the going is good.

Strategies for the Dominant Firms (Market Leaders)

The dominant business or market leader is one that has a relatively very high share of the market in a particular industry Kotler, (1994) suggests the following strategies for dominant firms (Market Leaders).

(a) Keep the Offensive strategy: Dominant firms can keep the marketing offensive and competitive pressure on their business followers by pursuing and investing in innovation, cutting prices whenever necessary and generally assuming the role of leadership in all phase at all times. The scheme insists that the leader keeps pushing for increased market share, without giving competitors a chance to strengthen up. The leader must be efficient and innovative without being contended.

(b) Use Confrontation Strategy: The leader should be prepared to beat the competition in advertising and in price. Ward off all price challenges of smaller firms by meeting or beating their prices. (c) Fortification Strategy: Introducing individual brands to compete with own company's successful brands. Keeping the competitors from entering the market. As an alternative you can protect your products' technology or patents. Coca-cola has done this well; only three people at any one time know Coke's formula.

(d) Maintenance Strategy: In the event that the leader simply wants to maintain its current level of market domination, it can simply keep its production capacity, operating efficiency, promotional budgets etc at their current level and try to bring about a stable market condition (Nnedu, 1996). The dominant firm sets objectives under this strategy for the firms market position and then maintain investment accordingly, using excess cash flows to support business growth. In all, the dominant firm or market leader faces three challenges, expanding the total market, protecting market share, and expanding market share. The market leader seeks to expand the total market because it is the chief beneficiary of any increased sales (Kotler, 1994 and Enyioko, 1999).

Strategies for Challengers in the Industry

A challenger must first define its strategic objective in the industry. Some of the strategies enunciated by Kotler and Singh, (1981) to be used by challenger include:

- (a) Attacking the leader strategy: This is a high-risk strategy but potentially high pay off strategy and makes good sense if the leader is a false leader; and not serving the market well. The alternative strategy is to out innovate the leader across the whole segment.

- (b) Attacking firms of the same size strategy: Firms of the same size that are not doing the job and are under-financed could be attacked. Consumer satisfaction and innovation potential need to be examined minutely. Even a frontal attack might work if the other firms' resources are limited.

- (c) Attacking small local and regional firm strategy: Equally small local and regional firms that are not doing the job and are under-financed could be attached. Several of the major beer company grew to their present size not by stealing each other's customers but by gobbling up the smaller firms.

(d) Other attack strategies available to challengers include:
- Price discount
- Cheaper goods/services
- Prestige goods
- Product/Service innovation
- Improved services
- Distribution innovation
- Manufacturing cost reduction
- Intensive advertising/promotion
- Customer conviction to use products/services
- Improvement of product/service quality Enyioko, 1999).

Strategies for the Followers in the Industry

Many runner up firms prefer to follow rather than challenge the market leader. Levith, (1966: 63) says that "innovation imitation might be as profitable as a strategy of product innovation". Market follower must know how to hold current customers and win a fair share of new customers. Each follower tries to bring distinctive advantage to its target market-location, service and financing. The follower has to define a growth path, but one that does not invite competitive retaliation. Three broad strategies for followership are distinguished hereby Kotler, (1994):

(a) Cloner Strategy: In this strategy the cloner emulates the leaders products services, distribution, advertising and others- pattern. The cloner does not originate anything but parasitically lives off the market leaders investment. In extreme, the cloner is a counterfeiter who produces 'knock off' of the leader's products or services- using 'me too' strategy.

(b) Imitator Strategy: The imitator copies some things from the leader but maintains differentiation in terms of packaging advertising, pricing and so on. The leader does not mind the imitator as long as the imitator does not attack the leader aggressively.

(c) Adapter Strategy: The adapter taken the leader's products and adapts and often improves them. The adapter may choose to sell different materials to avoid direct confrontation with the leader.

Nicher Strategies

An alternative to being a large market is to be a leader in a small market or a nicher. Smaller firms normally avoid competing with larger firms by targeting small markets of little or no interest to the larger firms (Kotler, 1994).

The strategic requirements and characteristics for an ideal

niche business according to Newman et al, (1985) include:

- Specialization
- High volume low cost
- Sufficient size and purchasing power that will lead to high profit ability
- High level of growth potential
- Favourable strength in resources
- Being of negligible interest to major competitors
- Favourable and distinctive skills
- Distinctive research and development

In his works, Kotler (1994: 403) defines a market nicher as " a small firm that chooses to operate in some specialized part of the market that is unlikely to attract the larger firm". The special roles open to market nicher ie (marketing strategies for Nicher) highlighted by Kotler (1994) include:

- ♦ End-user specialist: The firm specializes in serving one type of en-user customer. For example a law firm can specialize in criminal or civil case or a hospital can specialize in eye treatment or dental matters.
- ♦ Customer-size specialist: The firms concentrates on serving either small, medium size or large customers
- ♦ Specific-Customer specialist: The firm limits its selling to one few major customer.

- Geographic specialist: The firm sells only in a certain locality or region
- Service Specialist: The firm offers one or more services not available from other firms.
- Product or Product line Specialist: The firm produces only one product line or product.
- Channel specialist: The firm specializes in serving only one channel of distribution.
- Vertical-level specialist: The firm specializes at some vertical level of the production-distribution value chain.

Other Conventional Corporate Strategies

There are other conventional strategies that are used by organisations to sustain their survival propensities. Such strategies are discussed below under the conventional corporate strategies, they include:

a) Conventional Strategy: This strategy emphasises the concentration of business investment on a single type of business. The strategy encourages consistency and uninterrupted practice on a given line of business so that the practitioner will be perfect with immense experience as he would be regarded as a 'guru' in the line. There is efficiency of operation due to specialisation in a conventional line of business (Enyioko, 1999).

b) Vertical Integration Strategy: Vertical integration strategy is used to spread risks along the operating continuum from raw materials supplies to the outlet of finished product sales, (Nnedu, 1996). This strategy involves acquiring one or more of the supplies to gain more profit on control – backward integration, (Kotler, 1994).

c) Growth or Market Opportunities Strategies: There are many ways in which an organisation can gain market shares or sustain growth rate profiles. Writers like Ansoff, (1965), Markin, (1979), Kotler (1994), and Waterman Jr. (1982) seem to agree on major classes for growth or market opportunities/strategies. Table 6.2 shows the major growth or market opportunities that could lead to three major growth strategies, namely intensive, integrative and diversification growth strategies.

Table 6.2: Major Classes of Growth / Market Opportunities.

1. Intensive Growth	2. Integrative Growth	3. Diversification Growth
♦ Market Penetration	♦ Backward Integration	♦ Concentric Diversification
♦ Market Development	♦ Forward Integration	♦ Horizontal Diversification
♦ Product Development	♦ Horizontal Integration	♦ Conglomerate

Source: Adapted from Kotler, (1994, P.77) Marketing Management Analysis, Planning, Implementation and Control 8th Ed. New Jersey: Prentice Hall.

From the presentations in table 6.2 we have seen that a company can fill its strategic marketing plan gaps in three strategic ways as follows:

(1) Intensive Growth Strategy: In this strategy the firm reviews whether there are any further opportunities for improving the performance of its existing businesses. The first assignment under this strategy is to identify untapped opportunities

that could help the firm achieve strategic growth with its current business arrangement , (Enyioko, 1999). Ansoff, (1957:114) has proposed a useful framework for detecting new intensive growth strategies called product/market expansion grid shown in table 6.2.

Figure 6.1: Ansoff's Product/Market Growth Matrix or Product/Market Expansion Grid (with three intensive growth strategies)

	Current Products	New Products
Current Market	1. Market penetration Strategy	3. Product Development Strategy
New Market	2. Market Development Strategy	4. Diversification

Source: Adapted (with minor amendment) by the authors to sooth the environment from Ansoff (1957: 114) "Strategies for Diversification" Harvard Business Review Sept. – Oct.

From the presentations in table 6.3 (an extension of Intensive growth strategy, three additional strategies have emerged as follows:

Marketing Strategies and Strategic Marketing

1(i) Market – Penetration Strategy: In this strategy, management looks for ways to increase the market share of its current products in their current markets.

(ii) Market – Development Strategy: With this strategy, the organization finds or develops new markets for its current products.

(iii) Product Development Strategy: With this strategy the organization develops new products of potential interest to its current market.

2. Integrative Growth Strategy: Through effectively investigating possible integration moves the organization can discover additional sources of sales volume increase over time. The integrative growth strategy could be achieved through backward, forward or horizontal integration strategies.

    (i) Backward Integration or Vertical Integration Strategy (already discussed see 2.8(b)

    (ii) Forward Integration Strategy: Acquiring some wholesalers or retailer who are profitable into the business

    (iii) Horizontal Integration Strategy: Acquiring one or more competitors into the business provided that the Government does not bar the move (Kotler 1994).

3. Diversification Growth Strategy: Diversification Growth Strategy is more meaningful if good opportunities can be found outside the present business. According to Kotler (1994: 78) "a good opportunity; --- is one where the industry is highly attractive and the company has the mix of business strengths to be successful". Three types of diversification strategies include:

(i) Concentric Diversification Strategy: In this strategy, the organization seeks new products that have technological and /or marketing synergies with existing product line, even though the product may appeal to new class of customers.

(ii) Horizontal Diversification Strategy: The company that decides to search for new products that could appeal to its current customers through technologically unrelated to its current product lines is applying horizontal diversification.

(iii) Conglomerate diversification Strategy: In a conglomerate diversification strategy the organization seeks new businesses that have no relationship to the company's current technology, products, or markets.

Effective Strategy Implementation

The design and formulation of a strategy do not guarantee successful business operation without considerations to its effective implementation. It is one thing to develop clear and meaningful strategy, it is another matter to implement it effectively. Koontz (1980:294) outlined basic requirements for effective strategy implementation as follows:

- Strategies should be communicated to all key decision-making managers

- Planning Premises must be developed and communicated

- Action plans must contribute to and reflect major objectives and strategies

- Strategies should be regularly reviewed.

- Consider developing contingency strategies and programmemes

- Make organisation structure fit planning needs

- Continue to reach planning and strategy implementation

- Create a company climate that forces planning

The development, communication and implementation of strategy are the most important activities of top managers. Ross and Kami (1973: 132) have maintained that: Without a strategy the organisation is like a ship without a rudder, going around in circles. It is like a tramp, it has no place to go.

In essence, they ascribed most business failures to lack of strategy, or wrong strategy or lack of implementation of a reasonably good strategy. They concluded that "without an appropriate strategy effectively implemented, failure is a matter of time" (Koontz et al, 1980: 281).

The implementation of a strategy successfully is a major programmeme of the organisation. Therefore, in order to successfully or effectively implement a strategy, management/leadership of the company has to create an appropriate organisational structure and capable staff consistent with the internal resources and external environment of the organisation Nnedu (1996). Once the firm has organised itself to carry out its strategy and has developed action plans and budgets, it can begin implementations. This starts by managing the activities of various members of the organisation as they put the action plans into operations. Schewe (1987:588) insists that:

> Implementation requires careful delegation of responsibilities, coordination of the work of different individuals and departments, effective communication, and motivation in the form of good leadership and reward system.

This means that proper implementation of strategy requires that managers take all these responsibilities seriously and keep them in mind at all times.

For effective implementation of a company's strategy Mckinsey (Waterman, 1982:12) developed strategy implementation framework known as Mckinsey's 7-Ss Framework or strategic- feat. See figure 6.2

Figure 6.2: Mckinsey's 7-Ss Framework

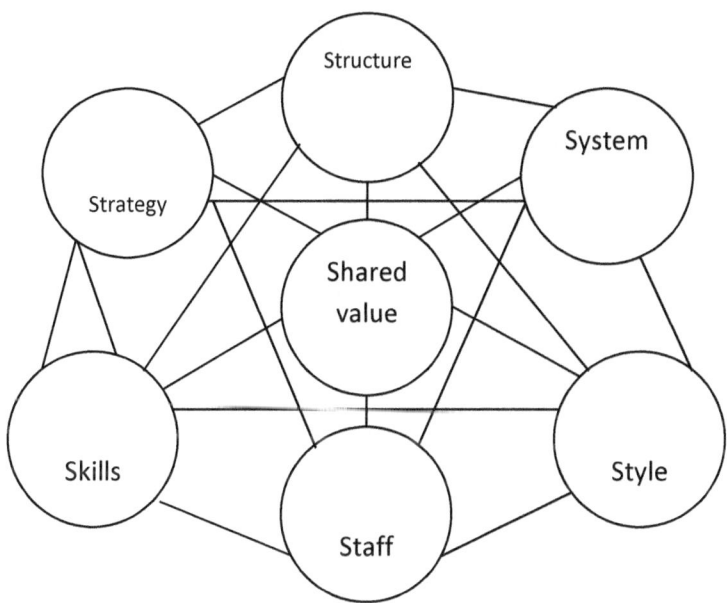

Source: Waterman and Peters, (1982: 12) In search of Excellence: Lessons from Americans Best Run Companies. New York: Harper and Row.

The Mckinsey's seven Ss framework (strategic management fit) shown in figure 6.1 states that strategy is formulated, implemented and controlled in that order and in a very segmented manner. However, strategy proceeds incrementally, and the political realities of most organisations demand that many strategists and non strategists alike accept a strategy before it can be implemented (Waterman et al 1982). Fubara (1996: 21) opines that :

> at the centre of implementation of a strategy is the shared value of the organisation. What does that mean? In the more developed country, management schemes, the shared value of an organisations at the centre of an organisation strategy and the nerve centre linking all the aspects of the seven Ss. It determines the corporate destiny, it is shared by nearly all, understood by all and believed by all. The effect is successful implementation.

The powerful actors that would perfect successful implementation of strategy have been encapsulated in Mckinsey's framework. According to Fubara (1996) they are made up of people involved with Mckinsey's seven Ss known as strategy, structure, skills, systems, staff, style and shared value (see figure 6.2). These elements are found in the internal organisational environment.

- Strategy: This is a coherent set of action aimed at gaining a sustainable advantage over competition, improving position vis-avis customers or allocating resources

- Structure: The organisation chart and accompanying baggage that show who reports to whom and how tasks are both divided and integrated.

- Systems: The processes and flows show how an organisation gets things done from day to day (information systems, capital budgeting systems, manufacturing processes, quality control systems, performance measurement systems).

- Style: Tangibles evidence of what management considers important by the way it collectively spends time and attention and uses symbolic behaviour (what managers say is less important than the way they behave)

- Staff: The people in the organisation (here it is very useful to think not about individual personalities but about corporate demographics.

- Shared Values: (or super-ordinate goals). The values that go beyond, but might well include, simple good statements in determining corporate destiny, (to fill the concept, these values must be shared by most people in an organisation.

- Skills: A derivative of the rest (skills are those capabilities that are possessed by an organisation as a whole as opposed to the people in it (Waterman and Peters, 1982).

The appropriate and effective use/harnessing of Mckinsey's 7Ss frame work rooted on share value loyalty and adequate communication arrangement will allow for effective strategy implementation in a marine industry.

Service Organisations and their Strategies

Many authorities and institutions have ventured into finding the true meaning of services and how it should be classified and conducted efficiently to achieve satisfactory result. According to Pride, et al, (1985 : 262), a service "is an act performed by an individual or organization for the benefit of another individual or organization". The American marketing Association (Glossary, 1960) defines service as "activity, benefit or satisfaction which is offered for sale or is provided in connection with sale of goods". Kotler, (1994) defines service as "any or performance that one party can offer to another that is essentially intangible and does not result in the ownership of anything. Its production may or may not be tied to a physical production"

Hornby, et al, (1971) define service as "Something done to help or benefit another or others". In his own definition, Okafor, (1996) says that service is an identifiable and intangible activity which provides want-satisfaction that is not tied to the production or the sale of a tangible product or another service. Grouping services, Okafor, (1996) classifies services into, professional services, personal services, rentals, entertainment services and general services. Graven, (1982) classifies services under two broad categories namely; consumer services and producer services.

Kotler, (1994) characterizes services as intangible, inseparable, variable, and perishable. Busch et al, (1985) while highlighting the strategic issues in marketing of services maintain that there are similarities in marketing of product and services. However, the characteristics of services call for different considerations when applying strategic factors. They also identify the major characteristics of services as:

i. Intangible: Services are not physical products they cannot be seen, tested, felt, heard or smelled before they are bought. Levitt, (1981) insists that service providers task is to "manager the evidence to tangibilize the intangible" because of this characteristics. Kotler, (1994) maintains that for service organization to tangilize the intangible it needs positioning strategy and in consideration to the tools of place, people, equipment, communication, symbols and price,

ii) Inseparability: Service are typical produced and consumed simultaneously. If service is rendered by a person, the provider is part of the service.

iii) Variability: Services are highly variable, since they depend on who provides them and when and where they are provided. Service buyers are aware of this high variability and frequently talk to others before selecting a service provider.

Hamermesh, (1984) says that the best ways to harmonise variability and maintain quality control in service business are:

(a) Investing in good personnel selection and training,

(b) Standardising the service –performance process throughout the organization and

(c) Monitoring customer satisfaction through suggestion and complaint systems, customer surveys and comparison shopping, so that poor service can be detected and corrected.

iv) Perishability: The reason many doctors charge patients for missed appointments is that the service value existed only at the point when the patient should have shown up. Service cannot be stored.

Schwartz, (1981), describes several strategies for producing better match between demand and supply in service business. They include:

- Different pricing
- Cultivation of non peak demand through good scheduling
- Provision of alternative service through complements

- Managing the demand level through reservation systems on the supply side.
- Hiring of part time employees to serve peak demand
- Introduction of peak-time routines
- Encouraging increased consumer participation
- Developing shared service system more especially in Telecom.
- Developing facilities for future expansion.

Table 6.3: Understanding of the Service Act

What is the Nature of the Service Act?	Who or What is the Direct Recipient of the Service	
	People Services directed at people's bodies	Things services directed at goods and other physical possessions:
Tangible actions	Health care Passenger transportation Beauty salons Exercise Clinics Restaurants haircutting	Freight transportation Industrial equipment repair and maintenance Janitorial services Laundry and dry cleaning Landscaping/lawn care Veterinary care
Intangible actions	Services directed at people's minds: Education Broadcasting Information services Theatres Museums	Services directed at intangible assets: Banking Legal services Accounting Securities Insurance

Source: Christopher H. Lovelock, "Classifying services to Gain Strategic Marketing insights," Journal of Marketing, vol. 47 (Summer 1983:12).

One way of viewing services is based on the object that is being served whether it is people or things. (see Table 6.3) when the service is performed on people, the customer must be present – either physically, as in the case of aerobic class, or mentally, as in the case of an educational service. If the customer is present, satisfaction is more likely to be determined by the interaction with service personnel. In addition, convenience and location become more important when the customer's presence is required. Contrast this with the situation represented by a credit card sender – generally the only contract is through a mailed monthly statement.

Creatively envisioning the nature of service can open up opportunities. By studying the classification scheme and where ones product fits into it, a marketer can create new approaches to providing satisfaction. Consider the service provided by educational institutions. Since the customer's physical presence is not needed, many universities now offer some courses in which students in many locations watch a class on public television, read the text, and take examinations either by mail or by visiting the campus on a few occasions. (Schewe, 1987:255)

Strategic Options for Service Organisations

The marketing strategies for service organizations are not very different from those involved in physical product; however, there are minor complexities that come as a result of the nature and the characteristics of service. In view of these complexities Gronroos, (1984) argues that service marketing requires not only external marketing but internal as well as interactive marketing (see figure 6.3).

Figure 6.3: Three Types of marketing in service Industries

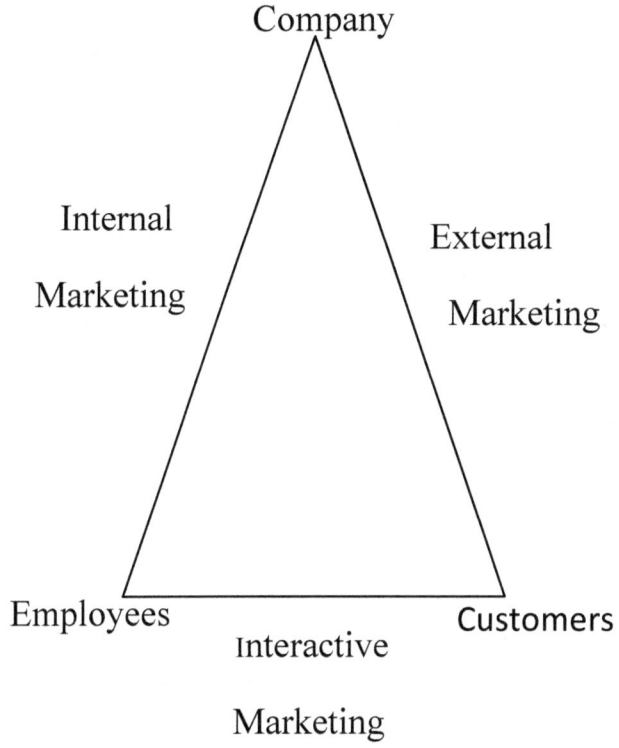

Source: Adapted from Kotler, (1994:470) Marketing Management Analysis, Planning, Implementation and Control

External marketing describes and the normal work done by the company to prepare, price, distribute and promote the service to customers.

Internal marketing describes the work done by the company to train and motivate its employees to service customers well. Berry, (1986) argues that the most important contribution the marketing department can make is to be "exceptionally clever in getting everyone else in the organization to price marketing"

Interactive Marketing describes the employees' skill in serving the client. The client judges service quality not only by its technical quality (e.g, was the surgery successful?), but also by its functional quality (e.g. Did the Surgeon show concern and inspire confidence?) Philip Kotler and P. N. Bloom (1984) insist that professionals along with other service providers must deliver high touch" as well as 'high technology.

Various studies have shown that when service companies manage their competitive differentiation, service quality, and productivity well they achieve high result. Therefore the key strategic feats for the service organization centre around the three areas outlined, (Berry and Parasuraman 1991). Firnstahl, (1989) maintains that excellent service organization apply the following strategies.

    i)   Setting of High Standards: The best service providers set high service quality standards. The standards must be set appropriately high

ii) A Strategic Concept: Service companies are 'customer obsessed". They have a clear sense of their target customers and the customer needs they are trying to satisfy; and they develop distinctive strategies for satisfying them.

iii) Satisfying the employees as well as the customers: Excellently managed service companies believe that employees relation and welfare will in turn lead to good customer relation and treatment. Management of such organization creates the environment for employee support and rewards for good service performance.

iv) System for Satisfying Complaining Customers: Very effective service organizations respond quickly and generously to customer complaints.

v) Top-Management Commitment to Quality: Top management of service companies do not look only at the financial performance of the organization on monthly bases but also on service performance. (Heskel et al, 1990).

vi) System for monitoring Service Performance: Top service firms audit service performance, both their own and competitors' on regular basis. They use a number of devices to measure performance comparison; shopping, ghost shopping, customer surveys, suggestion & complaints forms, service-audit teams, and letters to the Direct of the organization. (Gravens, 1982).

CHAPTER 7

MARKETING (MIX) STRATEGIES

Once an organisation has finished formulating its objectives including the marketing objectives its next step is to develop marketing strategies that would enable it achieve its marketing and overall objectives.

Marketing strategy is "a series of integrated actions leading to a sustainable competitive advantage" (John, 1971:98). The marketing strategy or plan is the central instrument for directing and coordinating the marketing effort. Therefore, companies or organisations that want to improve their marketing effectiveness and efficiency must learn how to create and implement sound marketing strategy (Kotler, 1994).

Leonard, (1990) insists that marketing strategy highlights action plans on location, pricing, client interactions, promotions, delivery and product design of the firm. He says that marketing strategy asks answers questions about market segmentation/target, market penetration, market share and market positioning.

In Summarising the importance of marketing strategy, Bliss, (1970), says that if they are implemented conscientiously by active and efficient managers they should increase market share, increase sales and profit, better corporate image, good competitive profile, growth and high level of survival propensity.

Other benefits/importance of marketing strategy indicate that:

i. it specifies goals of action and expect development/outcome

ii. it eliminates surprises by giving systematic thought/guideline about the future.

iii. It forces decision makers to think through what action they would take if certain events should come through.

iv. It gives management the ability and direction to manage change.

v. Marketing strategy indicates the means of coordinating various corporate activities after analysing the advantages and the disadvantage available to a firm in a competitive situation and helps the organisation to achieve result.

vi. Marketing strategy strengthens an organisation as it gives it clearer vision for corporate thinking and better utilization of resources and increase probability of certainty of attaining marketing objectives. (Robert, 1994). Marketing strategies are better organised and analysed under the following subheadings

(i) Product strategy (ii) Pricing strategy (iii) Distribution strategy and (iv) promotional strategy.

Product Strategy

Product is the first and the most important element of the marketing mix. Product strategy calls for making coordinated decisions on product stages and lines (Kotler, 1980). At the product level the company should reformulate its marketing strategy several time. Not only do economic conditions change, and competitors launch new assaults but in addition, the product/service passes through various stages. Consequently a company must plan successive strategies appropriate to each state in the product/service life cycle. (Ansoff, 1969).

The product life cycle portrays distinct stage in the sale history of a productive/service. Corresponding to these stages are distinct opportunities and problems with respect to marketing strategy and profit potential. By identifying the stage that a product is or may be headed toward, companies can formulate better marketing strategies. (Kotler, 1994). The product/service life cycle stages include: (I) Introduction stage, (ii) Growth stage (iii) maturity stage and (iv) Declining stage

Marketing Strategies in the Introduction Stage

In launching a new product or service, the organisation can set a high or low level for each marketing variable, such as price, promotion, distribution and product/service quality. In the introduction stage of the product/service the firm can pursue any of the following strategies as shown in Table 7.1 (Kotler, 1994).

Table 7.1: Four Introductory Marketing Strategies

PROMOTION

	Level	High	Low
PRICE	High	Rapid, Skimming Strategy	Slow Skimming Strategy
	Low	Rapid Penetration Strategy	Slow Penetration Strategy

Source: Adapted from Philip Kotler, (1994) Marketing Management

As seen in Table 7.1, there are four strategies that the organisation can use at the introductory stage of the product/service, they are:

(i) Rapid Slimming Strategy – which consists of launching the new product or service at high price and high promotion level

(ii) Rapid penetration strategy consists of launching the new product at a low price and high level of promotion

(iii) Slow Skimming strategy consists of launching the new product/service at high price and low promotion

(iv) Slow-penetration strategy consists of launching the new product at a low price and low level of promotion.

In the introduction stage these strategies do not allow for high profits at times they bring negative profits because of the low sales and heavy distribution and promotion expenses. Much money is needed to attract distributors and fill the "pipeline". Promotional expenditures are at their highest ratio to sale because of the need for a high level of promotional effort to;

(i) Inform potential consumers of the new product/service.

(ii) Induce trial of the product and

(iii) Secure distribution in detail outlets (Buzzel, et al, 1987).

Marketing Strategies in the growth stage

During this stage, the organisation uses several strategies to sustain rapid market growth. They include:

- Improving product/service quality, adding of new features and improved styling

- Adding new models Entering new market segments

- Increasing its distribution coverage and entering new distribution channels

- Shifting from product-awareness and advertising to products/service-preference advertising

- Lowering price to attract the next layer of price-sensitive buyers

The firm that pursues these market expansion strategies will straighten is competitive position. (Kotler, 1994).

Marketing Strategies in the Maturity Stage: Most products/services are in the maturity stage of the life cycle, therefore, most of the marketing plan/strategies deal with mature products (Wasson, 1978).

Organisations systematically consider using strategies of market, product, and marketing mix modification. The

Market Modification: Involves the expansion of the market for the mature brand and increasing its volume by convincing current brand users. The organisation can expand the number of brand user in three ways:

(i) Convert non users: The company can try to attract non users to the product/service.

(ii) Enter new market segments: The company can try to enter new market segment- geographic demographic etc

(iii) Win Competitors customers: The company can attract competitors' customers to try or adopt the brand.

The organisation can increase the volume by convincing current band users to increase their annual usage of brand through: More frequent use, more usage per occasion, and new and more varied uses. (Weber, 1976).

Product Modification: Involves the organisation trying to stimulate sales by modifying the product characteristics which include quality improvement, feature improvement and style improvement.

Marketing mix Modification: The organisation can also try to stimulate sales by modifying one or more marketing mix elements.

Marketing Strategies in the Declining stage: In the declining stage an organisation faces a number of tasks and decisions to handle its aging products.

In a study of company strategies in declining industries, Harrigan, (1980), distinguishes five decline strategies available to the firm:

- Increase the firm's investment (to dominate or strengthen its competitive position)

- Harvesting (or milking) the firm's investment to recover cash quickly

- Maintain the firm's investment level until the uncertainties about industry are resolved.

- Decrease the firm's investment level selectively by sloughing off unprofitable customer groups, while simultaneously strengthening the firm's investment in lucrative niches.

- Divesting the business quickly by disposing of its assets as advantageously as possible.

Products/services have life cycles that call for changing marketing strategies over time. Every new need follows a demand life cycle that passes through the stages of emergence, accelerating growth, decelerating growth, maturity and decline (Kotler, 1978).

Pricing Strategy

According to Okafor, (1996) "Pricing Strategy considers a company's pricing setting procedures and methods relative to its product costs, market demand and competitive prices. A price strategy begins with a clear statement of objectives and ends, that need to be met with price". Price is the amount of money of exchange value needed to acquire something.

Price goes by many names, according to Schwartz, (1981: 271): *"Price is all around us. You pay rent for your apartment, tuition for your education, and a fee to your physician or dentist the airline, railway, taxi and bus companies charge you a fare; the local utilities call their price a rate, and the local bank charges you interest for the money you borrowed. The price of driving your car on expressway is toll, and the company that insures your car charges you a premium. The guest lecturer charges an honorarium to tell you about a government official who took a bribe to help a shady character steal due collected by trade associations. Clubs or societies to which you belong may make a special assessment to pay unusual expenses. Your regular lawyer may ask for a retainer to cover his / her services. The "price" of an executive is a salary, the price of a sales person may be a commission, and the price of a worker in a week is wage. Finally, although economists would disagree, many of us feel that income taxes are the price we pay for the privilege of making money".*

Price is a very sensitive element of the marketing mix because it is the only element that produces revenue, the other elements produce cost. Price is also one of the most flexible elements of the marketing mix. Pricing and price competition are the number one problems facing marketing executives (Kotler, 1994).

In effective pricing strategy, the organisation first of all has to decide on what it wants to accomplish with the particular product. If the company has selected its target market, and market positioning carefully, then its marketing mix strategy including price will be fairly straight forward, (Edelman, 1971). In setting the price of a product/service the organisation follows six step-procedures,

    (i)   The company carefully establishes its marketing objectives, such as survival maximum current profit, maximum current revenue, maximum sales growth, maximum market skimming or product quality leadership (Ogbowu, 1990).

    (ii)   The company determines the demand schedule, which show the probable quality purchased per period at alternative price levels (Bennet, et al 1974).

    (iii)   The company estimates how its costs vary at different output levels and with different levels of accumulated production experience

    (iv)   The company selects one of the following pricing methods: Markup, target return, perceived value, going rate and sealed bid pricing (Nimer, 1975).

(v) The company selects its final price, expressing it in the most effective psychological way.

Pricing strategies are best used to handle special situations. For example

- Government task force could threaten to investigate the company's pricing arrangement.
- A sizable firm may have fallen into a desperate financial situation so that it was forced to raise cash through a liquidation of its inventories.
- A large new firm may have entered the market
- Business may have fallen of precipitately for the entire industry etc.

Special situations like these require adjustment in price – the formulation of strategy is to guide management in setting price during the time that the special situation endures (Oxenfeldt, 1960). In pricing strategy, the firm must decide where to position its production on quality and price. The arrangement shows that the positioning levels of the products do not complete with each other, but only complete within each group. Yet there can be competition between price-quality segments (Kotler, 1994).

Marketing Strategies and Strategic Marketing

Table 7.2 shows nine possible price quality strategies:

Table 7.2: Nine Price/Quality Strategies

High	Medium	Low
1. Premium Strategy	2. High-Value strategy	3. Super-Value Strategy
4. Overcharging strategy	5. Medium Value Strategy	6. Good Value Strategy
7. Rip off strategy	8. False economy Strategy	9. Economy Strategy

Source: Adapted from Philip Kotler, (1994) Marketing Management Analysis Planning, Implementation and Control. Eight edition, New Jersey : Prentice Hall Inc.P.490

From Table 7.2 above, it is explained that the diagonal strategies 1, 5 and 9 can all coexist in the same market, that is, one firm offers a high quality product at a high price, another firm offers an average-quality product at an average price, and still another firm offers a low-quality product at a low price. All the competitors can co-exist as long as the market consists of three groups of buyers – Those who insist on quality, those who insist on price, and those who balance the two considerations. Positioning strategies 4, 7 and 8 amount to over pricing the product in relation to quality, (Kotler, 1994). It is very important that the organisation should constantly consider competitors reactions as well as the customer when effecting any pricing strategy.

Distribution Strategy

Distribution strategies are the intermediaries producers and organisations use to reach the final consumer in order to sell their products and services. As Kotler (1994:525) observes, distribution or marketing channel decision are among the most critical decisions facing management. "The company's chosen channels ultimately affect all the other marketing decisions." The place-component of the marketing mix addresses itself with specific attention to channel distribution system. Channel strategy is usually guided by customer location and customer preferences, the product characteristics, competitive behaviour and environmental constraints etc. Channel members as observed by Nnedu, (1996) are also members of the marketing team since they help in promotion, distribution, financing etc of the product and help to foster product and marketing strategies. Channel strategies vary from product to product. Marketing or distribution channels are viewed as "sets of interdependent organisations involved in the process of making a product or service available for use or consumption (Stern, et al. 1992:1).

A marketing or distribution channel performs the work of moving goods from producers to consumers. Kotler (1994), insisted that marketing channel overcomes the time, place, and possession gaps that separate goods and services from those who would use them. The functions performed by marketing channels include:

- Information: The collection and spreading of marketing information including Research and Development for the organisation. Also, the highlighting of facts and information leading to the tapping of potentially customers, and outwitting of competitors are normally supplied by the distribution channel in the first instance (Kotler, 1994).

- Promotion: The development, designing and dissemination of persuasive communications or promotion about the products and services of the organisation are equally performed by the marketing channels

- Bulk Breaking: A basic principle of distribution is to ship in large quantities the products. It then fall upon the shoulders of the channel distribution system to break the bulk, as wholesalers are highly noted for this.

- Risk bearing: When intermediaries take title to the products they sell, they take on the risks of damage, deterioration, obsolescence, etc (Schewe, 1987).

- Price Setting: Channel of distribution takes on the responsibility for pricing the product at various points in the distribution system.

- Management Services: Wholesalers for example, may help their retail customers with such projects as improving accounting techniques, improving in store promotional displays controlling inventory, and enhancing advertising and sales training as well as other functions.

• Financing: Intermediaries finance their customers through credit granting. In more specific areas, the wholesalers give their patronising retailer the opportunity of credit granting as they supply the products on credit.

Storage: The successive storage movement of physical products from raw materials to the final consumer. The wholesalers and retailers in particular keep their wares in their stores as they sell them from time to time.

Types of Distribution Channels

There are number of alternative routes through which products take before reaching the consumer. These networks of intermediaries constitute the distribution channel. Based on the objectives of the organization, its marketing objectives and other factors different avenues exist for the distribution strategies of products and service. Figure 7.3 shows typical distribution channels.

Marketing Strategies and Strategic Marketing

Figure 7.3: Types of Channel of Distribution

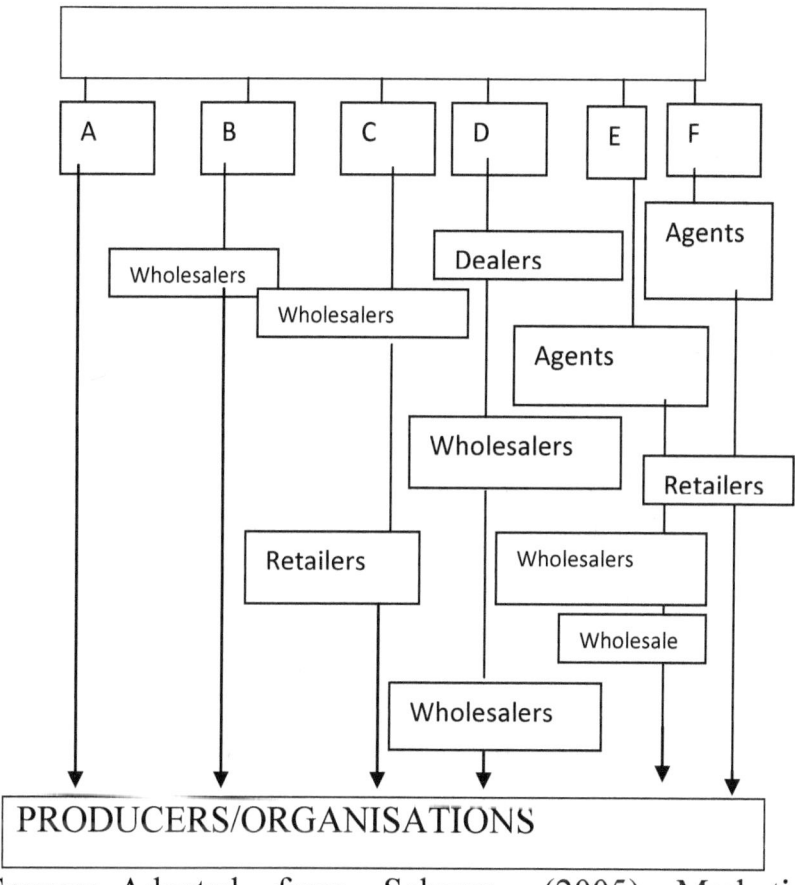

Source: Adapted from Schewe, (2005) Marketing Principles and Strategies. New York: London House Press. P. 394 with amendment to suit the objective of the Book.

Channel A: This is the quickest and easiest channel of distribution to manage as the producers sell directly to the consumer without any recourse to passing through the other intermediaries. It is "short and direct" channel since the product moves straight from the manufacturers or the organization to the final consumer.

Channel B: Channel B has one intermediary before the consumer. In this channel the wholesaler buys from the manufacturer and sells direct to the consumer. This channel is also shorter but not the shortest.

Channel C: This is the most channel applicable to many organizations. In this channel the manufacturing ships the goods to the wholesalers who store the products and break the bulk and thereafter sell to the retailers that finally sell to the consumers.

Channel D: This is a type of channel that recognizes the activities of dealers in the business. The manufacturers sell to the dealers who later sell to the retailers and retailers finally sell to consumers. This type of channel arrangement is applicable to oil distribution.

Channel E: This channel starts with Agents to wholesalers and from wholesalers to retailers and from retailers to the final consumer.

Channel F: Under this channel arrangement the manufacturer passes through the agents or dealers and straight to retailers and consumers.

Designing and Managing of Distribution Strategies

Designing and managing and distribution strategies involve examining several channel-decision problems facing manufacturers as they concern the determination of what is feasible what is ideal and what is available as they select, plan, modify, motivate and evaluate the channel alternatives, (kotler, 1994).

In fact, designing channel system as Kotler, (1994) opines calls for analysing customer needs, establishing channel objectives, identifying the major channel alternatives and evaluating them.

In analysing customer's need the procedure involves the understanding of what, where, why, when and how target customers buy as the first step. The marketer or the organisation must understand the service outlet, (Schewe, 1987). As outlined and highlighted by Bucklin, (1972) channels produce five service outputs as follows:

Lot Size: This is the number of units that the marketing channel permits a customer to buy on a buying occasion. The smaller the size, the greater the service output level that the channel must provide and accommodate.

Waiting Time: This is the average time that customers of that channel are expected to wait for the receipt of goods and services. In designing the channel of distribution it should be understood that customers prefer fast delivery channel to slow ones. In this case, faster service requires greater service output level for efficiency and effectiveness.

Spatial Convenience: Spatial convenience expresses the degree to which the marketing channel makes it easy for customers to purchase the product.

Service Backup: Service represents the incentive prone services (such as credit, delivery, installation, repair etc) being provided by the channel system.

Product Variety: Product variety represents the assortment packages being provided by the channel. Customers would normally prefer channels with varieties of assortment packages because it increases the chance of meeting their needs promptly, (Kotler, 1994).

Having designed the channel selection appropriately the next thing is to manage the channel effectively. The first step in channel management is the establishment of channel objectives which should be stated in terms of the targeted output level. Channel management involve coordinated activities that anticipate and understand the sources of channel conflicts, needs aspirations and problems and try to harmonise them accordingly (Schewe, 1987). It is to the advantage of each channel member if co-operation is sustained at all times so that the distribution objectives could be achieved. It should be more realistic if achievement channel objectives are established by the organisation.

The next thing after establishing channel objectives is the identification of major channel alternatives. The organisation should weigh the advantages and disadvantages of using its own sales force; manufacturers, agency, dealers industrial distributors, wholesaler or retailers to the final consumer. According to Kotler (1944:532), a channel alternative "is described by three elements, namely; the type of business intermediaries, the number of intermediaries and the terms and responsibilities of each channel participant. At this stage of determining channel alternatives, the length and the kind of intermediaries should equally be known. This is what is called "intensity of distribution". The intensity of distribution consists of three alternative namely; intensive distribution, selective distribution and exclusive distribution (Bucklin, 1972).

Incentive Distribution: I an "approach to distribution that seeks the largest possible number of outlets in given territory", (Schewe, 1987: 402).

Selective Distribution: Is an "approach to distribution that seeks the largest possible number of outlets in a given territory", (Schewe, 1987:402).

Exclusive Distribution: Is an approach to distribution in which the number of intermediaries is limited to one for each geographic territory (Schewe, 1982).

Having established and selected channel objectives/alternatives, the organisation should find the best arrangement for motivation of the channel members. They must be provided with motivational incentives coupled with training, supervision and general encouragement. In managing and motivating channel members Kotler, (1994) has identified five power bases for achieving a fit in channel management relationship. They include:

- Coercive Power: power threatening to punish the channel member or withdraw a resource or terminate relationship.

- Reward Power: Power of the manufacturer to offer extra benefit for better performance of middlemen.
- Legitimate Power: Rightful power wielded by the manufacturers on the middlemen requesting for certain behaviour as a result of ownership and relationship.
- Expert Power: Is applied by the manufacturer who has special knowledge that is valued by the middlemen.
- Reference Power: Occurs when the manufacturer of organisation is so highly respected that middlemen are found to be identified with him/it.

A further procedure in channel management is the evaluation and continuous control of the channel members. The producer must continuously be evaluating the channel members against certain criteria: Economic control and adaptive. Periodically, the organisation or manufacturer evaluates the performance of channel members with respect to standard of performance, sales quota attainment, average inventory levels, customer delivery time, treatment of damaged and lost goods, cooperation in promotional and training programmes.

Promotion Strategy

Promotion is any form of communication used by a firm or seller to inform, persuade or remind potential buyers about it products/services, images, ideas, etc. (Okafor, 1996).

According to Roman, (1989) marketing communication mix (also called the promotion mix) consists of five major tools:

- Advertising: Any paid form of non personal presentation and promotion of ideas, goods or services by an identified sponsor.
- Direct marketing: Use of mail, telephone, and other non personal contact tools to communicate with or solicit a response from specific customers and prospects.
- Sales promotion: Short term incentives to encourage trail or purchase of a product or service.
- Public relations and publicity: A variety of programmemes designed to promote and/or protect a company's image or its individual products.
- Personal selling: Face to face interaction with one of more prospective purchasers for the purpose of making sales.
- In developing effective promotional strategies eight steps are considered; namely:

(i) The communicator must first identify the target audience and its characteristics, including the image of the product.

(ii) Define the communication objectives, whether it is to create awareness, knowledge, like preference, condition of purchase.

(iii) Design a message containing an effective content, structure, format and source.
(iv) Communication channels – both personal and non personal must be selected.
(v) Total promotional budget must be established. Four common methods are the affordable method, the percentage of sales method, the competitive- parity method and the objectives – and task method.
(vi) The promotional budgets must be divided among the main promotional tools, as affected by such factors as push versus pull strategy, buyers readiness stage and product life cycle stage.
(vii) Monitor and see how the market becomes aware and tries the product and is satisfied in the process.
(viii) Communication must be managed and coordinated for consistency, good timing and cost effectiveness.

The type of promotion mix element to use at any time depends on the annual promotion budget, nature of the market, nature of the product and the products stage in its life cycle. The promotion budget may be determined by using any of the methods listed in (V) above, (Okafor, 1996). Kotler, (1994) lists common communication tools which could be used in promotional strategies as show in Table 7.3.

Table 7.4: Common Communication / Promotion Tools

ADVERTI-SING	SALES PROMO-TION	PUBLIC RELA-TIONS	PERSONAL SELLING	DIRECT MARKET-ING
Print and broadcast Adverts. Packaging-outer Packaging inserts Motion Pictures Brochures & Booklets Posters & Leaflets Directories Reprint of Adverts Bill Boards Display signs Points of Purchase displays Audio visual material Symbol or Logos	Contest, games, Sweepstakes, Lotteries Premium & Gift Sampling Fair & Trade shows Exhibits Demon-strations Couponing Rebates Low interest Financing Enter-tainment Trading stamps Tie	Press kits Speeches Seminars Annual reports Chain table Donations Sponsor-ships Publications Community Relates Lobbying Identity media Company Magazine Events	Sales Presentations Sales Meetings incentive programmes samples Fairs and Trade shows	Catalogues Mailings Television marketing Electronic shopping TV shopping

Source: Adapted from (Kotler), 1994 Marketing Management (p, 597).

Table 7.3 above shows most of the promotional tools under the five major promotional mix that could be used for effective design of communication/promotion strategies in any given organisation.

CHAPTER 8
STRATEGIC MARKET ORIENTATION, CUSTOMER VALUE AND SUPERIOR PERFORMANCE

To achieve superior performance, a business must develop and sustain competitive advantage. But where competitive advantage was once based on structural characteristics such as market power, economies of scale, or a broad product line, the emphasis today has shifted to capabilities that enable a business to consistently deliver superior value to its customers. A business is market-oriented when its culture is systematically and entirely committed to the continuous creation of superior customer value. Specifically, this entails collecting and coordinating information on customers, competitors, and other significant market influencers (such as regulators and suppliers) to use in building that value.

The three major components of strategic market orientation - customer orientation, competitor focus, and cross-functional coordination - are long-term in vision and profit-driven. Based on extensive interviews with managers and executives, Kohli and Jaworski (1990) conclude that strategic market orientation provides "a unifying focus for the efforts and projects of individuals, thereby leading to superior performance." A developing stream of empirical research has found a strong relationship between strategic market orientation and several measures of business performance, including profitability, customer retention, sales growth, and new product success.

Customer Orientation and Profitability

The heart of a strategic market orientation is its customer focus. To create superior value for buyers continuously requires that a seller understand a buyer's entire value chain, not only as it is today but also as it evolves over time. Buyer value can be created at any point in the chain by making the buyer either more effective in its markets or more efficient in its operations. A market-oriented business understands the cost and revenue dynamics not only of its immediate target buyers but also of all markets beyond, for demand in the immediate and "upstream" markets is derived from the demand in the original "downstream" markets. Therefore, a market-driven business develops a comprehensive understanding of its customers' business and how customers in the immediate and downstream markets perceive value. Employees of market-oriented businesses spend considerable time with their customers. Managers and employees throughout the business call on their customers or bring them into their own facilities in a constant search for new ways to satisfy their needs. For example, Du Pont has developed a programme called "Adopt a Customer" that encourages a blue-collar worker to visit a customer once a month, learn the customer's needs, and be the customer representative on the factory floor.

Market-driven businesses continuously monitor their customer commitment by making improved customer satisfaction an ongoing objective. To maintain the relationships that are critical to delivering superior customer value, they pay close attention to service, both before and after sales. Because of the importance of employees in this effort, these businesses take great care to recruit and retain the best people available and provide them with regular training. Some businesses even involve their customers in hiring, training, and developing contact people as well as in making motivation and reward system decisions. Involving customers in these key areas forges strong customer loyalty.

Competitor's Focus and Increased Sales Output
Creating superior customer value requires more than just focusing on customers. The key questions are which competitors, and what technologies, and whether target customers perceive them as alternate satisfiers. Superior value requires that the seller identify and understand the principal competitors' short-term strengths and weaknesses and long-term capabilities and strategies. For example, a team of Marriott employees traveled the country for six months, staying in economy hotels and collecting information about their facilities and services. Armed with this information about potential competitors' strengths and weaknesses, Marriott invested $500 million in a new hotel chain. Fairfield Inn, its budget market entry, achieved an occupancy rate 10 points higher than the industry average in one year.

A seller should adopt a chess-game perspective of its current and principal potential competitors. Moreover, it should continuously examine the competitive threats they pose, inferring these threats from intent and value-creation capabilities. This is crucial information to a seller in developing its contingency competitive strategies. In one case, Hewlett-Packard decided to accelerate the announcement of a new computer peripheral after discovering through its travel agency that a rival had booked conference rooms around the country for a specific date. Knowing that this rival had a similar product in development, H-P rushed its announcement and beat the competition to the market. In market-driven businesses, employees from all functions share information concerning competitors. For example, it is crucial for R&D to receive information acquired by the sales group about the pace of a competitor's technology development. Top managers frequently discuss competitors' strategies to develop a shared perspective on probable sources of competitive threats. A reason for the success of many Japanese companies is that they train managers to understand that competitive intelligence is part of everyone's job. Using this information, market-driven businesses often target opportunities for competitive advantage based on competitors' weaknesses. In any case, they keep competitors from developing an advantage by responding rapidly or anticipating their actions.

Inter functional Coordination and Superior Value

The third of the three core components of a strategic market orientation is the coordination of personnel and other resources from throughout the company to create value for buyers. Any point in the buyer's value chain is an opportunity for a seller to create value for the buyer firm. This means that any individual in any function in a seller firm can potentially contribute to value creation. As Michael Porter (1985) explains:

Every department, facility, branch office, and other organizational unit has a role that must be defined and understood. All employees, regardless of their distance from the strategy formulation process, must recognize their role in helping a firm achieve and sustain competitive advantage.

To accomplish this, effective companies have developed horizontal structures that focus on building value, such as time-to-market for new products. They manage projects through small multifunctional teams that can move more quickly and easily than businesses that use the traditional function-by-function, sequential approach.

For example, cross-functional teams call on customers to identify additional opportunities for value creation. Engineering becomes involved during preliminary market research to help marketers understand what is feasible. Production is involved during product design to ensure that the product can be manufactured at a reasonable cost. Engineers and production people constantly discuss their capabilities and limitations with sales and marketing so capabilities can be leveraged and limitations avoided when promoting products or services. When all functions contribute to creating buyer value this way, more creativity is brought to bear on increasing effectiveness and efficiency for customers.

Shapiro (1988) tells the anecdote of a company CEO explaining to top managers that because of increasing competition, the business needed to become more market-oriented. With that encouragement the marketing vice president jumped in, "I've been saying all along we need to be more marketing-oriented. Marketing has to be more involved in everything because we represent the customer and we have an integrated view of the company." At that point the CEO snarled, "I said more market-oriented, not marketing-oriented." That story is very representative of our experience with marketing orientation as well. A marketing orientation implies an emphasis on the marketing function that may not be appropriate. Customer value is created by core capabilities throughout the entire organization. Whereas Procter and Gamble's competitive advantage may be based on a core marketing capability, 3M's advantage is innovation; Canon's is technology. This does not make 3M or Canon any less market-oriented than Procter and Gamble. Because market-driven behavior permeates multiple functions at 3M and Canon, they may be more market-oriented and less marketing-oriented.

In the view, when a business achieves the objective of developing a pervasive strategic market orientation, the marketing function may become less - not more - important, because all functions are dedicated to creating and delivering customer value. This is consistent with Regis McKenna's (1991) notion that "Marketing is everything and everything is marketing."

Wiersema and Treacy, (1993) foresees a time when marketing specialists will become increasingly rare while marketing as a general management function becomes more important. This is the result of a general focus on cross-functional cooperation, which causes internal functional boundaries to lose meaning. However, for businesses that currently have an internal orientation on production or research and development, the marketing department may have to take the lead role in encouraging market-oriented thinking throughout the firm. As the primary boundary between the business and its markets, marketing is "management's window on the world" (Bower and Garda 1985). Because it is dependent on other functional areas for the timely and efficient development, production, and delivery of the product, marketing is likely to be the first function that fully appreciates the benefits of strategic market orientation. To maximize its effectiveness, marketing must demonstrate the benefits of market-driven behavior to top management and to other functions. Marketing may have a key role in the development and maintenance of a culture that is truly market-oriented.

The crux is that the responsibility for superior buyer value is beyond that of any one function. Creating value for buyers is analogous to a symphony orchestra in which all members contribute according to a general plan and in which the contribution of each subgroup is tailored and integrated by a conductor - with a synergistic effect. A seller must draw upon and integrate effectively all of its human and other resources in an ongoing effort to create superior value for buyers at a profit. This coordinated integration of company resources builds directly on both customer and competitor analysis.

From Strategic market orientation To Superior Customer Value: We argue that a market-oriented culture is necessary to build and maintain the core capabilities that continuously create superior customer value. Recent work in service management, quality development, and new product development points to the necessity of being market-oriented for success in these key strategic activities.

Quality Driven-Product and Customer Satisfaction

To deliver superior service, businesses must understand what their customers expect, for exceeding those expectations is the basis of enduring customer loyalty. Keeping an existing customer costs only about one-fifth as much as attracting a new one. As Kotler (1994) noted, "[Customer] defection is the worst thing that can happen." So to build customer loyalty, businesses must make a long-term commitment to understand their customers' expectations and how they change, motivate employees to view customer satisfaction as a primary objective, monitor customer satisfaction frequently, and stay in touch with customers after the sale.

Customer satisfaction is the most heavily weighted category in the Malcolm Baldrige National Quality Award. The examiners look for evidence of customer understanding, commitment, and impressive results. It has never been more true that quality must be defined by the customer. Achieving high quality requires continuously monitoring what customers want.

High quality and performance also require coordinating the work force so that such quality is an outcome of the design, production, distribution, and sales processes, with input from each function along the way. GTE's director of marketing resource development implies the importance of strategic market orientation as he describes the firm's progression from quality conformance to quality leadership: "Each stage increases the focus of a business on customer and market needs, with the final stage resulting in significantly enhanced business results" (Bruno 1992).

Innovation and New Product Development
In contrast to some "expert" opinions that new product success is the result of technology push, most of the research conducted in new product development over the past two decades shows that innovation and new product success are more likely to result from being market-driven. For example, Quinn (1986) found that all the innovative businesses he studied had a strong strategic market orientation and explicit mechanisms to force market-technical interaction. Based on four of their own studies, Waterman, Jr and Peters, (1982) identified "an in-depth understanding of the firm's customers and its marketplace" as the first factor in their model of new product development.

The academic research was supported by Fortune's finding that the most important characteristic of America's fastest growing companies is "putting the customer first - listening, understanding, serving" (Deutschman 1991). The success of these businesses is attributable to innovative new products, not just brand extensions, which can be lucrative without being very "new." For example, such recognized innovators as Monsanto, Coming Glass Works, and 3M consciously guide their development efforts into areas with the greatest commercial potential.

Developing A Strategic Market Orientation

Top management leadership is a necessity for the transition to a strategic market orientation. Because top managers often do not have firsthand experience with strategies or activities that build customer value, they must create an environment in which change can occur without specifically decreeing what that change will be. As Levit, (1983) explains: Probably the best way to maintain a path finding culture is, paradoxically, by not working at it - at least not directly - but rather by fertilizing the well-seeded soil that enables and nurtures [visionary] behavior, whenever and wherever it may develop. To accomplish this, senior management provides general guidelines for business unit managers on how the culture should change, empowering them to initiate and tailor customer value strategies. In addition, top management sets specific business unit standards for customer satisfaction and other measures of market performance. The role of top management is facilitative, deftly combining top-down strategy guidelines while encouraging bottom-up strategy insights and responsiveness. By communicating and discussing business unit successes with other units in the organization, top managers reinforce success and increase organizational learning. Most important, senior managers lead by example.

Alternative Approaches to Developing Strategic market orientation

There are two alternative strategies that businesses may apply to develop a strategic market orientation. The first, and more conventional, strategy is a "pragmatic" approach, outlined by Beer, Eisenstat, and Spector (1990), whereby managers attempt to implant the strategic market orientation "ethic" and culture directly. The philosophy underlying this approach is that organizational change is the result of changes in individual beliefs and behaviors. Therefore, the focus is on the attitudes and activities of individuals. Businesses that use a pragmatic approach to organizational change often adopt change programmes because they are fashionable rather than because management recognizes some intrinsic value in them. Management makes decisions and decrees actions because they are "correct" and fit the programme's philosophy. Organizational structures and administrative systems are modified as the foundation for future competitive efforts. Too often, consultants and staff experts take ownership of the programme and attempt to "convert" employees to the philosophy of strategic market orientation through training and communications. The programme's champions urge management and employees to have faith in the programme and to be patient about achieving results. The alternative is the "adaptive" approach. Under this approach, management and employees continuously learn from their efforts to create buyer value. They adjust strategy, structures, systems, and staffing based on such learning. Key performance measures are developed early and short-term performance improvement goals are set. Even though management has made a long-term commitment, the mood is one of impatience. Results of some sort are expected early in the programme; continuous improvement is expected throughout the programme.

Studies by Narver and Slater (1991) indicate that the adaptive approach is superior to the pragmatic approach for helping businesses become more market-oriented. Contrary to the fundamental assumption of the pragmatic approach, individual behavior is most effectively changed by putting people into new roles or responsibilities and empowering them to achieve results. In those new roles, individuals, functions, and businesses develop new understanding and appropriate capabilities in response to market results. The adaptive approach monitors results and then makes appropriate adjustments in the firm's structures and strategies. Moreover, the pragmatic approach is often too large-scale and diffuse precisely because it is not based on specific market problems. Assessing its effectiveness is difficult because of the abstractness of the specific problems. Because the pragmatic approach is often staff- and consultant-driven, it is neither "owned" nor supported by line workers.

Strategic Market Orientation and Continuous Learning

Market conditions and competitive threats never stand still. As the requirements for attaining a sustainable competitive advantage change, so must the particulars of the three core components of strategic market orientation. Strategic market orientation is not a preordained set of specific structures or behaviors. Rather, the three core components are manifested in the organization's culture and climate, and must be continuously adapted, as required, to create and maintain superior customer value within a given market. Ray Stata (1989), CEO of Analog Devices, warns that "the rate at which organizations learn may become the only sustainable source of competitive advantage."

The adaptive approach to developing and sustaining strategic market orientation is synonymous with organizational learning. Market-driven learning may be the only basis for creating superior value because, unlike products or technologies that may be obvious to competitors, it is a deeply embedded organizational process that is difficult for outsiders to perceive and almost impossible for them to imitate. A strategic market orientation is an externally focused business culture that makes creating superior value for buyers its top priority. That value comes from successfully exploiting core capabilities that can be developed in any functional area. But a strategic market orientation is far more than just a function of marketing. A marketing orientation results in placing the marketing function at the top of an organizational hierarchy, leading to a preoccupation with traditional marketing activities when they are neither the major nor the appropriate core capability of the firm. Just as with any functional primacy, a marketing orientation leads to internal conflict over resource allocations and business priorities. In addition, making any one function dominant denies the reality that superior customer value is created and maintained when all functions have the opportunity to contribute.

It is also important to resist the temptation to defer efforts to become market-oriented because of a favorable environment. Based on interviews with marketing and general management executives, Kohli and Jaworski (1990) found a pervasive belief that businesses could get away with being less sensitive to customers and competitors when a market was experiencing strong demand. In our research as well, we have found that the relationship between strategic market orientation and performance in high-growth, low-competition environments is slightly weaker than in low-growth, high-competition markets. In the long run, however, all businesses will encounter low growth and competitive hostility; these are the conditions that require a business to be market-driven. It is better to invest in developing a strategic market orientation while conditions are favorable than to wait until they are threatening. A business's opportunities for success will be maximized when all organizational members recognize that they can contribute to creating buyer value and are motivated and empowered to do so. Strategic market orientation is a culture that focuses their efforts and enables this to happen.

CHAPTER 9

MARKETING WARFARE STRATEGIES AND RELATIONSHIP MARKETING

Marketing warfare strategies are a type of strategies, used in business and marketing, that try to draw parallels between business and warfare, and then apply the principles of military strategy to business situations, with competing firms considered as analogous to sides in a military conflict, and market share considered as analogous to the territory which is being fought over(Levit, 1983). It is argued that, in mature, low-growth markets, and when real GDP growth is negative or low, business operates as a zero-sum game. One person's gain is possible only at another person's expense. Success depends on battling competitors for market share.

The Use of Marketing Warfare Strategies

Strategy is the organized deployment of resources to achieve specific objectives, something that business and warfare have in common. In the 1980s business strategists realized that there was a vast knowledge base stretching back thousands of years that they had barely examined. They turned to military strategy for guidance. Military strategy books like *The Art of War* by Sun Tzu, *On War* by von Clausewitz, and *The Little Red Book* by Mao Zedong became business classics.

From Sun Tzu they learned the tactical side of military strategy and specific tactical proscriptions. In regard to what business strategists call "first-mover advantage",

Sun Tzu said: "Generally, he who occupies the field of battle first and awaits an enemy is at ease, he who comes later to the scene and rushes into the fight is weary." From Von Clausewitz they learned the dynamic and unpredictable nature of military strategy. Clausewitz felt that in a situation of chaos and confusion, strategy should be based on flexible principles. Strategy comes not from formula or rules of engagement, but from adapting to what he called "friction" (minute by minute events). From Mao Zedong they learned the principles of guerrilla warfare.

The first major proponents of marketing warfare theories were Philip Kotler and J. B. Quinn.(1981) In an early description of business military strategy, Quinn claims that an effective strategy: "first probes and withdraws to determine opponents' strengths, forces opponents to stretch their commitments, then concentrates resources, attacks a clear exposure, overwhelms a selected market segment, builds a bridgehead in that market, and then regroups and expands from that base to dominate a wider field."

The main marketing warfare books were:

- *Business War Games* by Barrie James, 1984
- *Marketing Warfare* by Al Ries and Jack Trout, 1986
- Leadership Secrets of Attila the Hun by Wess Roberts, 1987

By the turn of the century marketing warfare strategies had gone out of favour. It was felt that they were limiting. There were many situations in which non-confrontational approaches were more appropriate. *The*

Strategy of the Dolphin was developed in the mid 1990s to give guidance as to when to use aggressive strategies and when to use passive strategies. Today most business strategists stress that considerable synergies and competitive advantage can be gained from collaboration, partnering, and co-operation. They stress not how to divide up the market, but how to grow the market. Such are the vicissitudes of business theories.

Marketing Warfare Strategies

- Offensive marketing warfare strategies - are used to secure competitive advantages; market leaders, runner-ups or struggling competitors are usually attacked
- Defensive marketing warfare strategies - are used to defend competitive advantages; lessen risk of being attacked, decrease effects of attacks, strengthen position
- Flanking marketing warfare strategies - Operate in areas of little importance to the competitor.
- Guerrilla marketing warfare strategies - Attack, retreat, hide, then do it again, and again, until the competitor moves on to other markets.
- Deterrence Strategies - Deterrence is a battle won in the minds of the enemy. You convince the competitor that it would be prudent to keep out of your markets.
- Pre-emptive strike - Attack before you are attacked.
- Frontal Attack - A direct head-on confrontation.
- Flanking Attack - Attack the competitor's flank.

- Sequential Strategies - A strategy that consists of a series of sub-strategies that must all be successfully carried out in the right order.
- Alliance Strategies - The use of alliances and partnerships to build strength and stabilize situations.
- Position Defense - The erection of fortifications.
- Mobile defense - Constantly changing positions
- Encirclement strategy - Envelop the opponents position. Cumulative strategies - A collection of seemingly random operations that, when complete, obtain your objective.
- Counter-offensive - When you are under attack, launch a counter-offensive at the attacker's weak point.
- Strategic withdrawal - Retreat and regroup so you can live to fight another day.
- Flank positioning - Strengthen your flank.
- Leapfrog strategy - Avoid confrontation by bypassing enemy or competitive forces Companies typically use many strategies concurrently, some defensive, some offensive, and always some deterrents. According to the business literature of the period, offensive strategies were more important that defensive one. Defensive strategies were used when needed, but an offensive strategy was requisite. Only by offensive strategies, were market gains made. Defensive strategies could at best keep you from falling too far behind.

The marketing warfare literature also examined leadership and motivation, intelligence gathering, types of marketing weapons, logistics, and communications.

Learning from Napoleon

To understand how business strategists use military strategies, we can look at the innovations of Napoleon and apply then to business situations. Napoleon made four key innovations. They were: 1) increase his army's marching rate, 2) organize the army into self contained units, 3) live off the country, and 4) attack the opponent's lines of supply. All four provide lessons for business strategists:

1) By increasing the speed that the army marched and fought, they created a military advantage. They could implement their tactics faster than the enemy. Hitler used the same strategy with his Blitzkrieg. The enemy was overrun before they were able to organize a viable resistance. But once these innovations were used, other armies made adjustments and the nature of warfare changed. All armies had to increase their pace of operations to be effective. Businesses, like armies must operate at a faster pace than their competitors in order to have a competitive advantage. They must develop and introduce products faster, implement strategies faster, and respond to environmental factors faster. They must be proactive.

2) Napoleon returned to the cohort organization of the Greek phalanx. These were self contained fighting units of citizens that knew each other in daily life, and had a wide variety of skills and various skill levels. Under the Roman Empire the phalanx was replaced by specialized legions containing 100 fighters (centurion). Each legion

had a specialized skill (such as the archer legions from Thrace). For more than 100 years, businesses have taken Adam Smith's advice and organized by functional specialization, just like the Roman legions did. Accountants populate the finance department and technicians populate the operations department. According to Adam Smith this is the most efficient way of organizing. But as the speed of business increases we need a more flexible system. We use cross functional teams (like the Greek phalanx) that have enough breadth of knowledge to see the big picture, are objective enough to get accurate and unbiased perceptions of environmental factors, and are flexible enough to act quickly.

3) Napoleon's armies lived off the country instead of bringing supplies with them. This allowed them to march faster. The disadvantage is that stealing from the local population created resentment. But this was a longer term problem. It could be dealt with when the time came. The short term advantage outweighed the long term disadvantage. In business we no longer stock inventory based on an EOQ model. We use a Just In Time model and this reduces costs considerably. However it makes us vulnerable to our supply channel partners. Just as Napoleon had to manage the local people that supplied him his provisions, businesses today have found supply chain management to be a critically important part of doing business.

4) Striking at the opponents lines of supply is known as a flanking strategy. It is effective because it eliminates the need to fight the enemy head-on. An attack on a poorly defended supply line can render the whole enemy army

unable to fight. In business today we attempt to do this with exclusivity agreements with suppliers (if you sell Pepsi, you can't sell Coke). If Pepsi has exclusivity agreement with Pizza Hut, Coke will effectively be eliminated from that part of the market.

Relationship Marketing

Relationship Marketing is an approach which emphasizes the continuing relationships that should exist between the organization and its customers. It emphasizes the importance of customer service and quality and of developing a series of transactions with consumers. The terminology was first described by Theodore Levitt in 1983.

Origin of the Relationship Marketing Approach

Already in 1980, B. Schneider wrote: What is surprising is that researchers and businessmen have concentrated far more on how to attract 'customers to products and services than on retaining customers. In 1983 Levitt wrote: In a great and increasing proportion of transactions, the relationship actually intensifies subsequent to the sale. This becomes a central factor in the buyer's choice of the seller the next time.

Relationship Marketing is strongly linked to Business Process Reengineering. According to this reengineering theory, organizations should be structured according to complete tasks and processes, rather than functions.

Usage of Relationship Marketing

Relationship marketing and traditional transactional marketing are not mutually exclusive and they are not necessarily in conflict with each other. Relationship

Marketing may be more suitable in the following circumstances or situations:

- High value products or services.
- Industrial products.
- Products are not generic commodities.
- Switching costs are high.
- Customers prefer a continuous relation.
- There is customer involvement in the production phase..

Steps in the Relationship Marketing Process

1. Chart the service delivery system. Set standards for each part of the system, especially the 'encounter points'.
2. Identify critical service issues.
3. Set service standards for all aspects of service delivery.
4. Develop customer communication systems.
5. Train employees on building and maintaining a good relationship with clients.
6. Monitor service standards, reward staff for exceeding service levels, correct sub-standard service levels.
7. Ensure that each employee fully understands the importance of quality and relationships in the marketing philosophy.

Strengths (Benefits) of Relationship Marketing

- Focus on providing value to customers.
- Emphasis on customer retention.

- The method is an integrated approach to marketing, service and quality. Therefore it provides a better basis for achieving
- Competitive Advantage.
- Studies in several industries show that the costs to keep an existing customer are just a fraction of the costs to acquire a new customer. So often it makes economic sense to pay more attention to existing customers.
- Long-term customers may initiate free word of mouth promotions and referrals.
- Long-term customers are less likely to switch to competitors. This makes it more difficult for competitors to enter the market.
- Happier customers may lead to happier employees.

Limitations of the Relationship Marketing model

Relationship Marketing is less appropriate in the following circumstances:

- Relatively low value products or services.
- Consumer products.
- Generic commodities.
- Switching costs are low.
- Clients prefer a single transaction to relationships.
- No / low customer involvement in production (Levit, 1983).

CHAPTER 10

PROFIT IMPACT OF MARKETING STRATEGY AND B2B MARKETING / DEFINTIONS

Profit Impact of Market Strategy (PIMS) database "yields solid evidence in support of both common sense and counter-intuitive principles for gaining and sustaining competitive advantage developed by Tom Peters and Nancy Austin. It was developed with the intention of providing empirical evidence of which business strategies lead to success, within particular industries. Data from the study is used to craft strategies in strategic management and marketing strategy. The study identified several strategic variables that typically influence profitability. Some of the most important strategic variables studied were market share, product quality, investment intensity, and service quality, (all of which were found to be highly correlated with profitability).

According to Lancaster, Massingham and Ashford (p531, Essentials of Marketing, 4th edition, 2002, McGraw Hill), PIMS seeks to address three basic questions:

- What is the typical profit rate for each type of business?
- Given current strategies in a company, what are the future operating results likely to be?
- What strategies are likely to help improve future operating results?

Dibb, Simkin, Pride and Ferrel (2001, p.677) cite six principal areas of information that PIMS holds on each business:

- characteristics of the business environment
- competitive position of the business
- structure of the production process
- how the budget is allocated
- strategic movement
- operating results.

Brief History of PIMS

The PIMS project was started by Sidney Schoeffler working at General Electric in the 1960s, then picked up by Harvard's Management Science Institute in the early 1970s, and has been administered by the American Strategic Planning Institute since 1975.

It was initiated by senior managers at GE who wanted to know why some of their business units were more profitable than others. With the help of Sidney Schoeffler they set up a research project in which each of their strategic business units reported their performance on dozens of variables. This was then expanded to outside companies in the early 1970s.

The initial survey, between 1970 and 1983, involved 2,600 strategic business units (SBU), from 200 companies. Today 3,811 observations exist; PIMS is managed by PIMS Associates in London. Each SBU give information on the market within which they operated, the products they had brought to market and the efficacy of the strategies they had implemented.

The PIMS project analysed the data they had gathered to identify the options, problems, resources and opportunities faced by each SBU. Based on the spread of each business across different industries, it was hoped that the data could be drawn upon to provide other business, in the same industry, with empirical evidence of which strategies lead to increased profitability. The database continues to be updated and drawn upon by academics and companies today.

Conclusion Drawn by PIMS

The original PIMS data survey led the PIMS project to identify 37 variables which account for the majority of business success. Two leading marketing texts differ slightly on which variables are the most important, with Dibb, Simkin, Pride and Ferrel (p676) identifying:

- a strong market position
- high quality of product
- lower costs
- lower requirement for capital investment

and Lanacaster, Massingham and Ashford (p.535) citing:

- market share
- investment intensity
- market growth
- life cycle stage
- marketing expense to sales ratio.

While many of these seem obvious, PIMS has the advantage of providing empirical data that define quantitative relationships and back what some may consider to be common-sense.

Participation in PIMS Study: Costs and Benefits

PIMS evaluated businesses' market position and suggest possible strategies, based on the data gathered from participating companies. Businesses wishing to use the service provide detailed information, including details of their:

- competitors and market
- balance sheet
- assumptions about future sales.

In return, PIMS provides four reports, described by Lancaster, Massingham and Ashford as:

1. A 'Par' report - showing the ROI and cash flows that are 'normal' for this type of business, given its market, competition, technology, and cost structure.

2. A 'Strategy Analysis' report, which computes the predicted consequences of each of several alternative strategic actions, judged by information in similar businesses making similar moves, from a similar starting-point and in a similar business environment.

3. A 'Report on Look-Alikes' (ROLA), which aimed at predicting the best combination of strategies for that particular company, by analysing strategically similar business more closely.

4. An 'Optimus Strategy' report, which is aimed at predicting the best combination of strategies for that particular company, again based on the experiences of other businesses in 'similar' circumstances.

Critique of PIMS

Clearly, it could be argued that a database operating on information gathered in the period 1970 - 1983 is outdated. However data continues to be collected from participating companies and PIMS argues that it provides a unique source of time-series data, the conclusions from which have proven to be very stable over time.

It has also been suggested that PIMS is too heavily biased towards traditional, metal-bashing industries, such as car manufacturing; perhaps not surprising, considering the era in which the majority of the surveys were carried out. In reality, as of 2006, the 3,800+ businesses contained within the database includes data from the consumer, industrial and service sectors.

It is also heavily weighted towards large companies, at the expense of small entrepreneurial firms. This resulted from the data collection method used. Generally only larger firms are prepared to pay the consulting fee, provide the survey data, and in return have access to the database in which they can compare their business with other large businesses or SBUs. Mintzberg (1998) claims that because the database is dominated by large established firms, it is more suitable as a technique for assessing the state of "being there rather than getting there". (page 99)

A serious theoretical criticism has also been mentioned. An empirical correlation does not necessarily imply causation. There is no way of knowing whether high market share caused the high profitability, or whether high profitability caused the high market share. Or even more likely, a spurious factor such as product quality could have caused both high profitability and high market share.

Tellis and Golder (1996) claim that PIMS defines markets too narrowly. Respondents described their market very narrowly to give the appearance of high market share. They believe that his self reporting bias makes the conclusions suspect. They are also concerned that no defunct companies were included, leading to "survivor bias".

Business-To-Business

Business-to-business, or "B2B," is a term commonly used to describe electronic commerce transactions between businesses, as opposed to those between businesses and other groups, such as business and individual consumers (B2C) or business and government (B2G).

B2B is also commonly used as an adjective to describe any activity, be it marketing, sales, or ecommerce, that occurs between businesses and other businesses rather than between businesses and consumers.

It is a term also used in electronic commerce and to describe automated processes between trading partners.

The volume of B2B transactions is much higher than the volume of B2C transactions. One reason for this is that businesses have adopted electronic commerce technologies in greater numbers than have consumers. Also, in a typical supply chain there will be many B2B transactions but only one B2C transaction, as the completed product is retailed to the end customer.

An example of a B2B transaction is a chicken feed company selling its product to a chicken farm, which is another company. An example of a B2C transaction is a grocery store selling grain-fed chickens to a consumer. B2B can also describe marketing activities between businesses, not just the final transactions that result from marketing, though the term can be used to identify sales transactions between businesses (also referred to as "institutional sales"). For example, a company selling photocopiers would more likely be a B2B sales organization than a B2C sales organization.

"Business-to-business" can also refer to all transactions made in an industry value chain before the finished product is sold to the end consumer.

Etymology of Business to Business

The term "business-to-business" was originally coined to describe the electronic communication relations between businesses or enterprises in order to distinguish it from the communications between businesses and consumers (B2C). It eventually came to be used in marketing as well, initially describing only industrial or capital goods marketing. However, today it is widely used to describe all products and services used by enterprises.

B2B Marketing Communications

B2B marketing communications is how businesses promote their products and services to other businesses using tactics other than direct sales. The purpose of B2B marketing communications is to support the marketer's sales effort and improve company profitability. B2B marketing is generally considered to be more complex than B2C marketing, as there is often more than one decision-maker involved in a B2B sale on the buyer's side.

B2B marketing communications tactics generally include advertising, public relations, direct mail, trade show support, sales collateral, branding, and interactive services such as website design and search engine optimization. The Business Marketing Association[1] is the trade organization that serves B2B marketing professionals. It was founded in 1922 and offers certification programmemes, research services, conferences, industry awards and training programmes.

B2B Marketing Methodologies

Positioning Statement

An important first step in business to business marketing is the development of your positioning statement. This is a statement of what you do and how you do it differently and better than your competitors.

Developing your messages

The next step is to develop your messages. There is usually a primary message that conveys more strongly to your customers what you do and the benefit it offers to them, supported by a number of secondary messages, each of which may have a number of supporting arguments, facts and figures.

Building a campaign plan

Whatever form your B2B marketing campaign will take, build a comprehensive plan up front to target resources where you believe they will deliver the best return on investment, and make sure you have all the infrastructure in place to support each stage of the marketing process - and that doesn't just include developing the lead - make sure the entire organization is geared up to handle the inquiries appropriately.

Briefing an Agency

A standard briefing document is usually a good idea for briefing an agency. As well as focusing the agency on what's important to you and your campaign, it serves as a checklist of all the important things to consider as part of your brief. Typical elements to an agency brief are: Your objectives, target market, target audience, product, campaign description, your product positioning, graphical considerations, corporate guidelines, and any other supporting material and distribution.

Measuring Results

The real value in results measurement is in tying the marketing campaign back to business results. After all, you're not in the business of developing marketing campaigns for marketing sake. So always put metrics in place to measure your campaigns, and if at all possible, measure your impact upon your desired objectives, be it Cost Per Acquisition, Cost per Lead or tangible changes in customer perception.

B2B Standards

UN/EDIFACT is one of the most well-known and established B2B standards. ANSI ASC X12 is a popular standard in North America. RosettaNet is an XML-based, emerging B2B standard in the high tech industry. An approach like UN/CEFACT's Modeling Methodology (UMM) might be used to capture the collaborative space of B2B business processes.

E-Marketplaces

"E-" or "electronic" marketplaces in a business-to-business context are primarily large online platforms (B2B portals) or websites that facilitate interaction and/or transactions between buyers and suppliers at organizational or institutional rather than individual levels. Since the builders of such marketplaces primarily aim at facilitating buyer-seller interaction (in most cases without being a buyer or seller themselves), these are also referred to as "third-party" B2B marketplaces. These marketplaces can do one or more of the following:

1. Help buyers find new suppliers and vice versa;
2. Help reduce the time and cost of interaction for B2B transactions;
3. Help increase trade between distant geographies;
4. Help manage payments and track orders for B2B transactions.

Vertical e-Marketplace

A vertical e-marketplace spans up and down every segment of one specific industry. Each level of the industry has access to every other level, which greatly increases collaboration. Buyers and sellers in the industry are connected to increase operating efficiency and decrease supply chain costs, inventories and cycle times. This is possible because buying/selling items in a single industry standardizes needs, thereby reducing the need for outsourcing many products.

Horizontal e-Marketplace

A horizontal e-marketplace connects buyers and sellers across many industries. The most common type of materials traded horizontally are MRO (maintenance, repair and operations) materials. Mainly business and consumer articles, these items are in demand because they are crucial to the daily running of a business, regardless of industry and level within that industry. Many corporations have MRO materials bought directly on-line by the maintenance team in order to relieve the purchasing department.

No-frills e-Marketplace

Developed in response to customers wanting to purchase products without service (or with very limited service), the no-frills e-marketplace parallels the B2C offering of no-frills budget airlines. The subject of several Harvard and IMD articles/case-studies, no-frills B2B e-marketplaces enable the effective de-bundling of service from product via clear "business rules." This provides the basis of differentiation from conventional B2B sales/purchasing channels.

Some Marketing Terms and their Definitions

Marketing Implementation Model   Marketing implementation model gives prototype and step by step guidelines on how a given market oriented design could be used to implement selected strategy for the achievement of marketing objectives. Some of the marketing implementation models involve:
(A) 1. Create Marketing Strategy
2. Create Marketing Implementation Programmeme (Use McKinsey 7S framework to include all aspects: Structure, Systems, Style, Staff, Skills, Strategy, Shared Values)
3. Implement Marketing Implementation Programmeme.
4. Monitor and adjust if necessary.
B) Compare also the marketing implementation process of Dibb, Sim Kin, Pride and Ferrel (2001):
1. Marketing strategy
2. Tactical decisions
3. Implementing the marketing mix (internal factors, external factors)
4. Monitor results
5. Adaptation of strategy/results.

Marketing Plan

A Marketing Plan is an annual plan of Marketing activities specifying Brand's revenue and expenditure. Key elements of Marketing Plans are: 1. Objective (Qualitative and Quantitative) 2. Calendar of Activities 3. Details of Expenditure etc. "it is an art and science of devising a way to sell the product, service, brand, the business unit, and even the entire company to meet customers' needs. Some may say identify the customers' needs first and then apply 4ps to deliver solutions ... whatever it is ... as long as your plan can sale then you make it. Time frame is a self-induce restriction.

Marketing a product/service is more an art than a science. People who lack creativity have made of marketing a science, so they can thrive. The essence of marketing is more like the Blue Ocean Strategy theory; the key is in the innovation (creativity), and that is not a science."

Marketing Planning

"Marketing planning needs to be integrated and coordinated with other planning activities. You need to do a marketing audit based on your corporate objectives and link this to your marketing objectives and strategies. It is a process of identifying and anticipating

Strategic Marketing	future events and aligning resources to meet the marketing objectives. In simple words, Strategic Marketing is a tool used to develop the Marketing Strategy of the company, in which case the gross strategic lines are followed by Operational Marketing issues. Strategic marketing is a verb and marketing strategy is a noun. It is reasonable to understand marketing strategy as a concept based and included on Mid Term Business Plan. Strategic marketing should be considered as a short term tactic inside marketing strategy. So, strategic marketing action should be considered for a better understanding.
Strategic Marketing Vs Marketing Strategy	Strategic Marketing is a planning process. Marketing Strategy is implementation of a strategy. "Strategic marketing is related to the corporate level for example CEO & Director, in which we allocate budget to each strategic business units (SBU), downsizing SBU etc. Marketing strategy is related to product manager level in which we create the marketing strategy for some product (for example price, distribution & promotion).

Strategic Marketing

Strategic Marketing would cover how an organisation intends to market its Brands, Product and Services, etc. In short, Strategic Marketing is at the Organisation Level and Marketing Strategy would be at the level of each marketing initiative". Strategic Marketing provides direction and analyses the market, competitors, customers and the capability of the organisation by focusing on geographic, demography and behaviour of customers. Marketing Strategy focuses on the company's products and their positioning in relation to sales-competition and customers.

Marketing Strategy Vs Strategic Marketing

The real question that needs to be answered is "what is strategy? ". Strategy, is a plan you device to differentiate all internal and external processes in your value chain, from your competition, with one clear outcome in mind. The outcome which the value chain should be tailored to achieve, is the corporate vision. Therefore marketing strategy, is a roadmap of how you plan to differentiate all activities which have an impact on the customer , in relation to the competitive environment, where the theme of differentiation is the corporate vision. Strategic Marketing is the process of continuously making alterations to the marketing strategy, with feedback from your external environment, as whichever strategic maneouvre you perform will alter your environment, thus the strategy itself needs to be re-adjusted.

Strategic Marketing versus Operational Marketing

"According to general literature strategic marketing is intended as a stage of analysis (of the competitive environment, of competitors, of firm's weaknesses and strengths, etc.) which is a premise to strategic decision related to the competitive positioning and, in general, to the mission of the firm. Operational marketing is devoted to implement the policies which should put the firm into the desired position. E.g.: customer's analysis and Porter's 5 forces analysis stand within the boundary of SM, while pricing and advertising stands within OM

AMA definition of Marketing

The American Marketing Association gives the following definition of marketing:
Marketing is the activity, set of

institutions, and processes for creating, communicating, delivering, and exchanging offerings that have value for customers, clients, partners, and society at large. So even AMA missed the point by Kotler, (1994), since their definition starts with creating the offerings, not with understanding the needs.

REFERENCES

Ahiauzu, A. I. (1981). "Towards a Diagnostic Approach to Motivating the Nigeria Workers" in Inauga ed. Managing Nigeria Economic System. London: Heinemann.

American Marketing Association Committee (1960). *Marketing Definitions: A Glossary of Marketing Terms.* Chicago American Marketing Association

American National Council of Physical Distribution Management (1969). *Marketing Definitions: Glossary of Marketing Terms.* Chicago: A.M.A. Press

Anderson, Paul F. (1982). "Marketing, Strategic Planning and the Theory Of The Firm", *Journal of Marketing,* 46 (Spring), 15– 26.

Ansoff, H. I. (1969). *Business Strategy.* Baltimore Penguin.

Appleby, R. C. (1969). *Modern Business Administration.* 2nd edition. London: pitman Books Ltd.

Appleby, R. C. (2001): *Modern Business Administration.* 8th Edition. London: Pitman's Press limited.

Bennett, S and Wilkinson, P. (1974). "Price – Quality Relationships and Price Elasticity under in-store. Experimentation". *Journal of Business Research* (January) pp 24-29.

Beer, M., R. Eisenstat, and B. Spector, (1990): "Why Change Programmes Don't Produce Change," Harvard Business Review, November-December (pp. 158-166).

Berry, L. L. and Parasuraman A. (1991). *Marketing Services: Competing through Quality.* New York: The Free Press.

Bliss, P. (1970). *Marketing Management and Behavioural Environment.* Engle wood-New Jersey: Prentice-Hall.

Bower, M and R.A. Garda,(1985) "The Role Marketing in Management," The McKinsey Quarterly,(Autumn , pp. 34-46.)

Bowerox, C. and Adler, L. (2003) "Symbolic Marketing". *Harvard Business.* November – December, p59.

Brown, S. (19980. "Post-Modern Marketing 2 - Telling Tales". *Thompson Business Press.*

Bruno, R.J. (1992):"The Evolution to Market-Driven Quality," Journal of Business Strategy, (September- October , pp. 15-20.)

Bucklin, L. P. (2001). *A Theory of Distribution Channel Structure*. California: University Press.

Busch, P. S. and Huston, M. J. (1985). *Marketing; Strategic Foundations*. Illinois: Richard Irwin

Buzzell, R. and Gale, B. (1987). *The PIMS Principles: Linking Strategy to Performance*, Free Press, New York.

Chandler, A. D. Jnr. (1962). *Strategy and Structure*. Massachussets: Massachussets Institute of Technology Press.

Corey, E. R. (2003). *Industrial Marketing Cases and Concept*. New Jersey: Prentice Hall.

Day, G.S. (1990): Market-Driven Strategy. New York: The Free Press,.

Day, G.S. and R. Wensley,(1988). "Assessing Advantage: A Framework for Diagnosing Competitive Superiority," Journal of Marketing, (April, pp. 1-20).

Day, G. (1994). "The capabilities of market-driven organizations". *Journal of Marketing*, 58 (October), 37–52.

Deutschman, A (1991). "America's Fastest Risers," Fortune, October 7, 1991, pp. 46-68.

Dickinson, R., Herbst, A. and O'Shaughnessy, J. (1986). "Marketing Concept and Consumer Orientation". *European Journal of Marketing*, 20 (10), 18–23.

Dibb, M; Simkin, Pride and Ferrel (2001). *Marketing Concepts and Strategies*, 4th Edition. European edition, Houghton Mifflin

Dierickx, I. and Cool, K. (1989). "Asset stock accumulation and sustainability of competitive advantage". *Management Science*, 35, 1504–11.

Doyle, P. (2000). "Valuing marketing's contribution", *European Management Journal*, 18 (3), 233– 45.

Drucker, P (1954). *Practice of Management*. London: Heinemann.

Drucker, P. (1965). *Practice of Management*. 2nd edition London: Heinemann.

Edelman, Franz, (1971). *Decision Making in Marketing*. New York: The Conference Board.

Ekwelibe, (1995). "Impact of foreign Exchange Regimes from the performance of Nigerian Economy (1962-1992)". *Unpublished MBA Thesis*. River State University of Science and Technology, Port Harcourt.

Enioto, O. F. (2004). "Distribution of Petroleum Products in Rivers State: The study of selected Oil Marketers in Rivers State" *A University Research Work*. Rivers State University of Science and Technology, Port Harcourt.

Enyioko, N. C. (1999). "Marketing Strategies of Hospital Service organisations in Nigeria – the study of Selected privately owned Hospital in Port Harcourt" *Unpublished MBA Thesis*. Rivers State University of Science and Technology, Port Harcourt.

Enyioko, N. C. (2005). "The Distribution Strategies of Bottling Companies in Nigeria: The Study of Nigerian Bottling Company Plc (Coca cola)". A University Research Work. Rivers State University of Science and Technology, Port Harcourt.

Enyioko, N.C. and Etim, P.C. (2006). "The Impact of Effective Marketing Strategies on Service Oriented Organisations in Nigeria : A study of Selected Firms in Port Harcourt". *Seminar Paper* Presented at Meridian Hospitals Limited Port Harcourt (March, 19)

Etuk, E. J. (1985). *The Nigerian Business Environment*. London: Macmillan Publishers.

Firnstahl, T.N (1989) "My Employees are My Service Guarantee" *Business Review* (July-August), PP29 34.

Fubara, B.A. (1983). "Government in Business" Management in Nigeria Lagos Vol. 19 No. 7 PP.28-33 (July).

Fubara, B.A (1996). "Business Policy, Corporate Strategy and the Realities of Management in Development Economies" *A Professorial Inaugural Lecture.* Rivers State University of Science and Technology, Port Harcourt.

Fubara, B. A. (1998) "Business Policy: Bus 648" *Lecture Notes.* Rivers State University of Science and Technology, Port Harcourt.

Garvin, D. A. (1987). "Competing on the Eight Dimension of Quality". *Harvard Business Review* (Nov-Dec), pp 101-105.

General Electric Company, (1952). *Annual Report.* New York: Prentice Hall.

Gorge, B. C. (1984). *The Effectiveness of Marketing Strategies in Services.* London: Pitman Publishing Co. Inc.

Gravens, D. W. (1982). *Strategic Marketing.* Illinois: Richard D. Irwin Inc.

Green, P.E., Tull, D.S. and Albaum, G (1993). *Research For Marketing Decisions,* 5th edition, Prentice-Hall

Gronroos, C. (1984), 'Internal marketing – theory and practice', in *The American Marketing Association 3rd Conference on Services Marketing, Services Marketing in a Changing Environment Vol. III.* Chicago: American Marketing Association.

Hambrick, D. C. and Fredrickson, J. W. (2001). "Are you sure you have a strategy"?. *Academy of Management Executive*, 15 (4), 48–59.

Hamermesh, R. G. (1984). *Making Strategy Work.* New York: John Wiley and Sons.

Harrigan, K. R. (1980). "Strategies for Declining Industries". *Journal of Business Strategy* (Fall, P. 51).

Harris, A.; Benneth N. and Preedy, M. (1997). *Organisational Effectiveness and Improvement in Education.* Buckingham: Open University Press.

Heskel, J. L. Sasser, W.E.Jnr., and Hart C.W.L. (1990). *Service Break Through.* New York: Free press Hollander S.C

Hornby, A. S, Gatenby, E. V. and Wakefield, H (1971). *Advanced Learners Dictionary of Current English, Sixth Impression.* London Oxford University Press.

John, S. (1971). *Marketing.* London: Pitman Press

Josey-Bass, M. (1988). *Riding the Waves of Change.* New Jersey: Mcgraw-Hill International.

Kerlinger, F.N.(1994). *Foundations of Behavioural Research,* 1st edition. Holt, Rinehart and Winston, p. 174

Kinear, T. C. and Root, A. R. (1989). Survey of Marketing Organisations, Foundations, Budgets and Compensation.

Kohli, A.K. and B.J. Jaworski,(1990). "Strategic market orientation:The Construct, Research Propositions, and Management Implications," Journal of Marketing, April 1990, pp. 1-18.

Koontz, H.; O'donnell, C. and Weihrich, H (1980). *Management. Seventh Edition.* Tokyo. Mc Graw Hill Book Limited.

Kotler, P and Singh, R (1981). "Marketing Warfare in the 1980" *Journal of Business Strategy* (Winter, pp 30-41)

Kotler, P.(1994). *Marketing Management: Analysis, Planning Implementation and Control Eight Edition.* New Jersey: Prentice Hall Inc.

Kotler, P (1994) "Marketing's New Paradigm: What's Really Happening Out There," Planning Review, September-October, pp. 50-52.

Kotler, P. (2002). *Marketing Management: Analysis Planning and Control* (8th Edition). Englewood Cliffs, NJ: Prentice Hall.

Kotler, P. (2005). *Marketing Management: Analysis, Planning, Implementation and Control* 9th *Edition.* New Jersey: Prentice Hall.

Lancaster, P; Massingham, R and Ashford, C (2002). *Essentials of Marketing, 4th Edition.* McGraw Hill), New York.

Leonard, P. C. (1990). *Principles of Marketing London.* Pitman Books Limited.

Levit, T (1966). "Marketing the Evidence in Intangible Product" *Harvard Business Review.* Vol.167 No116 pp33-41

Levit, T (1983). "The Marketing Imagination". *Harvard Business Review.* Vol.216 No. 58 pp42-55

Lloyd, C.J. (2002). "Industrialization and Economic Development in Nigeria: The Legal Perspective" *Unpublished Research Paper* .Rivers State University of Science and Technology, Port Harcourt.

Lovelock, C.H. (1983). "Classifying Services to Gain Strategic Marketing Insights" *Journal Of Marketing,* Volume 47; (Summer).

Maclayton, D. W (1998). " Basic Research Method Unpublished Monograph. Rivers State University of Science and Technology, Port Harcourt.

Mc Carthy, E. J., (1984). Basic Marketing; A Managerial Approach. Homewood Illinois: Richard D. Irwin

McCarthy, E. J., and Brogowkz, A. A. (1984). *Essentials of Marketing.* Homewood – Illinois: Richard D. Irwin, Inc.

McKenna, R. (1991): "Marketing Is Everything," Harvard Business Review, January-February (pp. 65- 79).

McKittrick, J. B. (1957). "What is the Marketing Management Concept?" In *The Frontiers of Marketing Thought and Science*, Frank M. Bass, ed., Chicago: American Marketing Association.

Mecimore, K.C. (2007). *Competitive Marketing Strategy: Technique for Analyzing Industries and Competitors.* London: Macmillan Publishing Company

Mintzberg, H. Ahlstrand, B. and Lampel, J.(1998). *Strategy Safari: A Guided Tour through the Wilds of Strategic Management.* The Free Press, New York.

Mitchell, C. (2002). "Selling the Brand Inside", *Harvard Business Review,* 80 (1), 99–105.

Moore, James F. (1993). "Predators and Prey". *Harvard Business Review* (May–June), 75–86.

More, P. R. (1986). *Marketing Techniques in Service Industries.* London: British Institute of Management.

Narver, J.C. and S.F. Slater, (1991): "Becoming More Market- Oriented: An Exploratory Study of the Pragmatic and Market- Back Approaches," Marketing Science Institute Working Paper, Report No. 91-128, October 1991.

Newman, W. H.; Logan, J.P and Hegarty, W. H (1985). *Strategy, Policy and Central Management 9th Edition.* Cincinnat: - Ohio South Western, Publishing Company.

Nnedu, E. E. I. (1996). *Business Policy and Strategy Management: Theory and Practice.* Port Harcourt: Para-graphics.

Nwachukwu, C. C. (1998). *Management Theory and Practice*. Onitsha: African Fepa Publishers Limited.

Nwala, C. (1978). "Turn Around Strategies in selected Nigeria Companies" *Management Journal* Vol. 22 No.8.

Ofobrukweta, M. U. (2001). *Shipping and Forwarding Practice-Imports* 2nd *Edition*. Lagos Fabolyn Nigeria Limited.

Ogbowu, B. E. (1990). "Marketing in Private Health Care Organisations: A Survey of Selected Private Health Care Organisations in Port Harcourt Metropolis. Port Harcourt: Rivers State University of Science and Technology, Port Harcourt.

Okafor, U. S. (1996). *Marketing Principles*. Owerri: African Educational Services.

Okwandu, G. A. (1998). "Sales Management" *Monograph on MKG 668*. Faculty of Management Sciences, Rivers State University of Science and Technology, Port Harcourt.

Osagie, P. C. (2005)."The Distribution Marketing of Petroleum Products in Nigeria: The Study of the Major Oil Marketing Companies in Nigeria." *A University Research Project*. University of Calabar, Calabar- Nigeria.

Osuala, E. C. (1997). *Introduction to Research Methodology* 2nd Edition. Onitsha Africana FEP Publishers Ltd.

Oxenfeldt. A. R. (1960). "Multistage Approach to pricing". *Harvard Business Review*. Vol. 38 (July-August) pp 125-133.

Oxfedeldt, A. R. and Moore, W. L. (1983). "Customer or Competitor: Which Guideline for Marketing?" In Stewart Henderson Britt, W. Boyd, Robert T. Davis and Jean Claude Larreche (Eds), *Marketing Management and Administration Action*. New York McGraw-Hill

Parasuraman, A.; Ziethand, V. A.; and Berry, L. L. (1985). "A Conceptual Model of Service Quality and its Implication for future Research" *Journal of Marketing* (Fall), pp 41 –50

Perreanet, W. D. Jr., and Frederick, A. R. (2002). "Physical Distribution Service in Industrial Purchase Decisions". *Journal of Marketing*. Pp 3-10.

Peteraf, M. A. (1993). "The Cornerstones Of Competitive Advantage: A Resource Based View". *Strategic Management Journal*, 14, 179–191.

Porter, M. E. (1980). *Competitive Strategy: Technique for Analyzing Industries and Competitors*. London: Macmillan Publishing Company.

Porter, M. E. (1985). *Competitive Strategy: Technique for Analyzing Industries and Competitors.* (2nd Edition) . London: Macmillan Publishing Company.

Prahalad, C. K. and Hamel, G. (1990). "The core competence of the corporation". *Harvard Business Review*, 68, 79–91.

Quinn, J.B. (1981). *Strategies for Change: Logical Incrementalism*, Irwin, Homewood Il

Quinn, J.B. (1986): "Innovation and Corporate Strategy: Managed Chaos," in Mel Horwitch, ed., Technology in the Modern Corporation: A Strategic Perspective (New York: Pergamum Press,).

Robert M. (1991). "The Resource-Based Theory of Competitive Advantage: Implications for Strategy Formulation", *California Management Review*, Spring, 118.

Robert, V. W. L, (1994). *A system for Managing Diversity*. Cambridge –Mass sett: Arthur D. Little (December)

Roman, E. (1989). *Integrated Direct Marketing.* New York: Mc Graw Hill

Ross, J. E. and Kami, M.J.(1973). *Corporation in Crisis Why the Mighty Fall.* Eagle Cliffs New Jersey: Prentice Hall Inc.

Schewe, D. S. (1987). *Marketing Principles and Strategies Marketing Principles and Strategies.* New York: Random House Inc.

Schewe, L. W., El-Ansa, A. I. (2000). *Marketing Principles and Strategies.* New York: London House Inc.

Schwartz, D.J. (1981). *Marketing Today: A Basic Approach.* New York: Harcourt Brace Jovanovich.

Shapiro, B.P. (1988): "What the Hell Is |Market-Oriented?'" Harvard Business Review, November-(December, pp, 119- 125).

Siropolis, N. C. (1994). *Small Business Management: A Guide to Entrepreneurship.* Boston; Houghton Migglin Company.

Stanley, S.F. and Narver, J.C (2010): "Strategic market orientation, customer value, and superior performance". Business Horizon, November 21 Feb pp.21-34

Stata, R. (1989): "Organizational Learning - The Key to Management Innovation," Sloan Management Review, Spring 1989, pp. 63- 74.

Slater, S.F. and J.C. Narver, (1994):"Does Competitive Environment Moderate the Strategic market orientation- Performance Relationship?" Journal of Marketing, (January, pp. 46-55).

Slatter, G (1984). "Effective Turn Around Strategies". *Harvard Business Review.* Vol. 21 No. 2 (Fall) pp21-43.

Stevenson, W. J. (2002). *Production / Operation's Management.* Illinois: Richard D. Irwin.

Straw G. C. (1998). *Human Asset Management.* New Jersey: McGraw Hill Inc.

Schoeffler, S. Buzzell, R. and Heany, D. (1974). "Impact of Strategic Planning on Profit Performance". *Harvard Business Review,* March-April, 1974.

Taylor, B. (1982). "Turn Around Recovery and Growth: The way through the Crisis" *Journal of General Management* Vol. 18 No. 2 (Winter) pp 5-13.

Teece, D. J., Pisano, G. and Shuen, A. (1996). "Dynamic Capabilities and Strategic Management". *Working Paper,* 53. Berkeley, CA: University of California Press.

Tellis, G. and Golder, P. (1996). "First To Market, First To Tail: The Real Causes Of Enduring Market Leadership". *Sloan Management Review.* Vol. 37, No. 2.

Thompson, Jr, A. A. and Strickland, A. J. III (1996). *Strategic Management* (9th Edition). Chicago: Irwin

Waterman, R. H., Jr and Peters, T. J. (1982). *In search of Excellence Lesson From America Best Run Companies.* New York: Harper and Row.

Wasson, C. R. (1978). *Dynamic Competitive Strategy and Product Life Cycle.* Texas: Houston Press.

Weber, J. A., (1976). *Growth Opportunities Analysis.* Virginia Reston Publishing Co.

Wiersema, F and Treacy, M (1993). "Customer Intimacy and other value Disciplines" Harvard Business Review (Jan-Feb) pp 84 –105).

Wilson A (1972). Product Policy Concept Methods and Strategy Massausett: Addison Wesley.

ABOUT THE AUTHOR

NEWMAN CHINTUWA ENYIOKO (B.Sc., MBA, M.Sc., MNIM)

Newman Enyioko hails from Umuopara Amuzu in Obi Ngwa Local Government Area of Abia State and lives in Port Harcourt, Rivers State, Nigeria. He had his primary school at Umuaro in Obi Ngwa LGA of Abia State and secondary school at Aba and Calabar, Nigeria . He studied Management and obtained a B.Sc. degree from the University of Calabar. He had his Masters (MBA) degree in Marketing from the Rivers State University of Science and Technology, Port Harcourt and another Masters (M.Sc.) degree in International Economics and Finance from the same University. He has worked as a Manager with Niger Optical Services Company Nigeria Limited, Port Harcourt and lectured (Research Methods, Operations Research, Marketing Management and Strategic Management) at University of Calabar, Port Harcourt Centre. Presently, (at the time of publishing this Book), he is the Research and Development Director of Medonice Management Consulting and Research Institute, Port Harcourt, Nigeria. He has written many articles in Local, National and International Journals. He is a prolific writer and author of many books and articles including: The Healing Power in the Word of God, Urbanization, Career Choice and Child Neglect in Nigeria, Impact of Government Expenditure on Nigerian Economy, The Role of NGOs in Sustainable Development, Business / Marketing Strategies of Health Maintenance Organisations (HMOs) in Nigeria , Human Resource Management and Performance Optimisation in Nigerian Universities, The Mystery of Holy Communion, Strategic Management Plans of Small Businesses in Nigeria: A University Research work), Problems of Small Business Management in Nigeria (The study of Selected Small Businesses in Aba: A University Project work), Sources of Finance for Business/investment (A Research work), Marketing Strategies of Hospital Service Organisations in Port Harcourt (The Study of Selected Hospitals in Port Harcourt: An MBA University Thesis), The Learning Organisations & the Society (A Research work), Sales Force Motivation in a Balanced Organisation (A Research work), Resources Planning and Management (An Empirical Study on Commercial Banks in Nigeria), The profound Effect of Consolidation / Mergers on Bank Recapitalization in Nigeria (A Research work), Evaluation of the Performance of the Millennium Development Goals (MDGs) in ECOWAS Countries: A Study of Nigeria and the Republic of Benin (An M.Sc. Thesis) and Global Poverty Reduction Strategies of Developing Economies. He is married with two children.